INDIAN NATIONALISM

INDIAN NATIONALISM:

ITS PRINCIPLES AND PERSONALITIES

BY

B. C. PAL

GYAN

Published by

GYAN

Gyan Publishing House
5, Ansari Road
Daryaganj, New Delhi-110002
Phone: 011-47034999, 9811692060
E-mail: books@gyanbooks.com

Distribution Network
gyanbooks.com
India, USA, Canada, UK, Australia, France

ISBN: 978-81-212-8232-1 (PB)
First Published, 1918

2nd Impression 2023

Printed at: Gyan Press, Delhi.

INDIAN NATIONALISM
Author: B. C. PAL

INDIAN NATIONALISM

INDIAN NATIONALISM:

ITS

PRINCIPLES

AND

PERSONALITIES

INDIAN NATIONALISM:

ITS PRINCIPLES AND PERSONALITIES

BY

B. C. PAL

S. R. MURTHY & CO.

TRIPLICANE, MADRAS, S.E.

FOREWORD

The Sketches published in this Volume were written from time for the periodical press and do not pretend to be in any sense an exhaustive study of all sides of the persons with whom they deal. This insufficiency will be specially noticed in the Sketches of the two most eminent of the leaders of Indian thought treated here namely, Mr. Tilak and Sir Rabindra Nath. Both the Sketches were written at the call of particular occasions, and do not, therefore, present their subjects, in all their aspects. To remove this defect, I would have to entirely rewrite these Sketches, which was not feasible and would not fit in with the limited scope of the present Volume.

Bhowanipore, Calcutta,
November 1918. } BEPIN CH. PAL.

CONTENTS

SIR RABINDRA NATH TAGORE

There is ample reason for congratulation in the award of this* year's Nobel Prize for Literature to Babu Rabindra Nath Tagore. Rabindra Nath is unquestionably the greatest among living men of letters in Bengal. He is perhaps the greatest in all India. Competent critics of his poems, who are equally conversant with contemporary literature in Europe and America, do not hesitate to assign him a high place among the very highest of contemporary poets in the modern world. Those who have so far received this Nobel Prize have no reason, therefore, to be ashamed of Rabindra Nath's company, though Rabindra Nath's people may justly think that he has every reason not to feel exactly flattered by being classed with one or two of these. Personally this Nobel Prize can confer, I think, no real honour on Rabindra Nath. Intrinsically, this recognition is of little value indeed, either to the poet himself

* 1913

or to his people, because it is not based upon a thorough acquaintance with his works, and is no testimony really, therefore, to his superior worth. Impersonally, however, it is of very great significance. This is the first time that a non-European literature has received such frank recognition from a body of distinguished European men of letters. It shows that the old and stupid barriers of ignorance and conceit have commenced to fall down even in Europe. To the non-Bengalee peoples of India itself, this European recognition will prove the wonderful advance that the Bengalee language and literature have made in less than a century and a half. As a people's literature is the surest sign and covenant of their culture, this appreciation of the work of the Bengalee poet, Rabindra Nath, by a body of men whose claims to represent the high-water mark of modern European culture will not be questioned, must establish the claims of the Bengalee people to a very superior culture and civilisation, even in the eye of modern Empire. This will be bound to indirectly raise the culture and civilisation of India as a whole, in the regard and esteem of the modern man. It will gradually help the growth of a true moral and intellectual *entente* between India and Europe, without which the present conflict of civilisation between the East and the West will never be satisfactorily solved. All these are matters of no small moment either to Indian Nationalism or to Universal Humanity. This Nationalism means, in its truest and sanest sense, the inviolable right of the composite Indian people, to fully and freely live its own special life in its own way, following its own peculiar genius, and developing its specific culture to its highest perfection, and thus to contribute what is highest and best in it, to the general stock of human knowledge and human culture. To establish this claim before the bar of modern humanity Indian Nationalism must prove that it has valuable elements in its special iife and culture, which, it would be to the profit of the rest of the world, to know, to study, and to assimilate. In other words, Indian Nationalism must prove, before it can command the ear of the modern world, that it has a message for them. Babu

Rabindra Nath has done this, to some extent, during his recent visit to Europe, on behalf of his country and his culture. That he has a message for his times, has been frankly acknowledged by many an English man of letters and leader of thought. And it has been proclaimed to all the world by the Academy of Literature of Stolkholm, who made the Nobel award. All these are, undoubtedly, very legitimate grounds for congratulation.

In our present mental and moral state, there is, however, very considerable risks of creating false and fanciful values, by these self-congratulations, whether they are personal and direct or impersonal and vicarious. Nor can it be denied that the jubilation over the award of the Nobel Prize to Babu Rabindra Nath, has distinctly developed this unhealthy tendency in many quarters. People have not cared to critically discriminate between the intrinsic and the extraneous value of this award. The congratulations to the poet by many of his people, have been marked by an utter absence of right perspective, and a lamentable lack of national dignity. Every school of Bengalee thought and every section, almost, of the educated Bengalee community, had united in rendering public homage to Rabindra Nath, as the undoubted sovereign head of the Bengalee literary world, upon the completion of his fiftieth year, in 1911. Rabindra Nath has given us nothing new since then. The Nobel Prize has, therefore, no intrinsic value to Rabindra Nath's own people, as a certificate of his work and worth. Yet the way that this Prize has been appraised in some quarters, clearly lends itself to the interpretation that it is a fresh sign and covenant of Rabindra Nath's greatness. Those who, by their foolish conduct and conversation, have been lending their support to this false estimate and interpretation of the Nobel award, have been simultaneously wounding our national self-respect and offering a positive insult to the poet himself. There was, no doubt, a time quite within living memory, when the hall-mark of European approbation determined very largely the market value of Indian achievements. Europe was then our highest standard of measurement. We liked then to think of our own great men in the terms of European greatness. Kalidas was, in those days, spoken of as the Shakespeare of India. Bankim Chandra, our greatest novelist, was the Sir Walter Scott of Bengal. Rabindra Nath did not escape the honour, and was lovingly called the Bengalee Shelly. But the new national awakening of the last few years had commenced to completely repudiate all these false and fanciful values. And no one had repudiated these with greater authority or effect than Rabindra Nath himself. He has been the first and the greatest leader of our intellectual and moral revolt against this soul-killing domination of European thoughts and ideals. It was Rabindra Nath, who, like Moses among the Israelites, first led his people out of their intellectual and moral bondage to Europe. And like Moses, Rabindra Nath must be very sorely troubled in spirit to find them repeatedly hankering still after the fleshpots of their old serfdom. And that Rabindra is still his own and proper self, and has taken an absolutely correct measure of this Nobel award, is completely proved, it seems to me, by the very candid, though somewhat inhospitable, reply that he made to the wild address of congratulation presented to him by the Bolepur Deputation.

Short as that reply was, and absolutely devoid of all literary embellishments, it was, to my mind, the best that we have had from Rabindra Nath for many a day past. Here it was not the poet flirting with soft and elusive ideas and catching them in fine and rapturous phrases, responding to their many moods with his many poses, who stood out in this address; but only the naked man and the indignant prophet, writhing in the anguish of his soul at the sight of the idolatry of his beloved people, who came and stood in all his native majesty before us. I remember to have seen the same man and the prophet in Rabindra Nath only once before, in his unregenerate days, when he stood in the Hall of the late Babu Pashupati Nath Bose's house at Bagbazar. It was the same Rabindra Nath who appears to have stood at Bolepur, pouring his soul out in righteous anger, before the assembled deputation. And the message that he delivered to his people, though clothed in a different language, and pitched in different tunes, was really the same. It was:—"Know yourself, honour yourself and help yourself, unmindful of both the smiles and the frowns of an unillumined and sympathetic world." Sympathy he had, and adulation too, in abundance, during his recent sojourn in England and America. No Indian has been more appreciated in those foreign lands. He facilitated them by his presence, hypnotised them by his personality, soothed them by the vague fragrance of his poesy, half sensuous and half supersensuous, which appealed, therefore, with irresistible power to people who, having almost a surfeit of the most refined sense-enjoyments, still found their hearts hungry and their spirits starved. Men gave him their prays, and women their adoration. But he knew the worth of it all. Rabindranath knows the value of ignorant adulation as much as that of ignorant neglect or contempt. The latter did not hurt him before and the former could not intoxicate him now. The way that some of his people took this European honour of their own poet, must have at first surprised Rabindra Nath, and then caused him great pain. It proved the failure of his highest and best mission among his own people. It was evidently with this pain gnawing at his heart that he came to receive the address of the Bolepur Deputation.

That address was couched indeed, in such terms, that it could not possibly fail to wound the inherently refined susceptibilities of Rabindra Nath, who is perhaps the most fine-fibred of our representative men. One of Nature's own aristocrats, Rabindra Nath can never stand the boisterous vulgarity of mob-admiration. Every thing that is loud treads upon his nerves. He once made a most determined attack on "Exaggerations." The exaggerations of this address was therefore bound to irritate his feelings. True genius always knows what it can and what it cannot do. It is fully conscious of both its superior strength and its inevitable weaknesses. Genius is, therefore, at once extremely audacious and extremely humble. Rabindra Nath as a man of very superior genius is as fully conscious of his powers as of his limitations. He could not bear to be told, therefore, even in a congratulatory address that his poetic productions had run the whole gamut of "Universal Human emotions"; and that he had reproduced in his divine lyre or the endless melodies of the 'choir invisible.' Rabindra Nath is not only a great poet but also a past master of prose style, superior to most, and inferior to no Bengalee writer whether living or dead. And the very style of this address, with its loud and barbarous array of rythmless sound, must have offended his keen literary sense, however much it essayed to please him by its fulsome adulation. And the cumulative effect of all this irritation due to a combination of many causes, came out in the ill-concealed bitterness of his short reply. No man of Rabindra Nath's position and sensibilities could have been less bitter under similar circumstances. Yet bitter as it undoubtedly was, the rebuke of his reply was neither undeserved nor undignified. He plainly told the deputation of the evident unreality of the demonstration they had got up in his honour. He knew that only a small percentage of those who formed that motley assembly had cared to read his works or had studied to understand his message. He must have seen before him others who had hitherto refused to give him their literary allegiance. And he asked them bluntly:—"What brings you gentlemen, here to-day? you, whom I had failed to please so long, what have I done, pray, now to please you so mightily? It is my worth, but the recognition of the foreigner, that has evidently worked up this sudden outburst of appreciation. I thank you for your generosity; but excuse me please, if I refuse to get drunk with you over this gilded cup of foreign wine." And Rabindra Nath would not have been what he is if he had failed to administer this salutary rebuke to those who evidently looked up still to European appraisers for the determination of the intellectual or moral values of their rational efforts and achievements.

But what must have pained and offended Rabindra Nath most deeply, in this address of congratulation, was, I think, its complete insensibility to what he had done in Europe. The address talked of his lofty genius, and his unique poetic achievements, as if these had any vital reference to the Nobel Prize. He wanted no new recognition of these at least from his own people. Any commendation of these by those who made the Nobel award, was worthless, for it could not have been possibly based upon any direct and competent knowledge of his works. The address referred to his deep mysticism, in the curious word, DHYANARASIK, especially invented by the writer for the occasion;—but even if he can at all claim the distinction, that too was very poor praise for one who represents Hindu culture. Every howling dervish in India and every roving religious mendicant would be counted as a mystic in Europe. And even if Rabindra Nath be a true mystic, a European certificate of his mysticism would hardly be worth citing in India. The Nobel Prize is significant only as a recognition of the success of Rabindra Nath's mission and the worth of his message, to Europe. Rabindra Nath would have been pleased to have some recognition of these from his own people also. This is, however, what he has not as yet found anywhere in all these public congratulations, upon his selection for this year's Nobel Prize for literature.

Indeed, there are very special reasons why Rabindra Nath would very naturally desire some such recognition from his own people. It is notorious that they did not quite like his idea of going out of the country for an indefinite sojourn among foreigners, when his inspiration and co-operation were specially needed by them in so many directions. New fields of work were opening out on every side under the impulse of the new spirit of nationalism in the country. The rejuvenescent life and energy of this ancient people were seeking fresh outlets in every department of their public activities. Practically denied free movement in politics, by the restrictive laws and regulations of the Minto regime, the new National ferment has commenced to organise itself in various movements of social advance and consolidation, and, more particularly, in new literary and educational efforts. Rabindra Nath's presence and guidance were especially needed for the due organisation and direction of these efforts towards their legitimate fulfilment. There was no one else in the country who could take his place in the leadership in these activities. For good many years past Rabindra Nath had been not only the greatest poet of Bengal, but also one of the most powerful and respected among the leaders of her public life. It is not true to say that for a time he was seduced by the Nationalists, as some Anglo-Indian scribes have been pleased to proclaim, to justify, as it were, the recognition which he has been recently receiving from high officials both in London and Simla. But he was really one of the creators of this new Nationalism itself. Before the birth of this nationalist movement in Bengal, Rabindra Nath was the poet of the English educated Bengalee only. By his contributions to this new nationalism, and especially through his new national-songs, Rabindra Nath at once became the poet and the pet of all Bengal; and his songs spread far and wide into the obscure corners of the province, and were sung by women in their zenana and recited by naked cow-boys under the shade of banyan or kadamba trees on the village common. The Nationalists did not lead Rabindra Nath astray, but it was Rabindra Nath who gave many of them their idea and inspiration of this new Nationalism. He is one of the chief, if not the chief, makers of this nationalism. The fact need not be denied now to save official appearances but should rather be proclaimed from the house stocks to prove official magnanimity. But like many other nationalist leaders of Bengal, what Rabindra Nath wanted was only a moral protest against the domination of foreign ideals and institutions, and he never councelled or countenanced any physical revolt against constituted state authority in the country. He was, at the most, like many of us, in those days, only a passive resister preaching practically the same gospel of resistance through suffering and sacrifice, which Mr. Gandhi has been preaching in South Africa. But the moment he saw that his ideal was being misunderstood, and the inspiration of his patriotism was being prostituted to revolutionary ends, Rabindra Nath, like many others, gradually fell away from an agitation that he found difficult to direct, and sought as far as he could, to put the brake upon it from the outside.

And it was here that people were forced to clearly realise the inherent limitations of the mind and character of their great leader. While Rabindra Nath's poems had established his reputation as the greatest of Bengalee poets after Vidayapati, Chandidas, and other creators of Vaishnavic lyrics; his prose essays had secured a very high position for him as a great original thinker also. By his superb style, his illuminating imagination, his intuitive insight into the very soul of things, Rabindra Nath had always stood head over shoulders above his contemporaries not only in Bengal, but, I think, in all India. All these are however the universal qualifications of superior poetic genius. They are hardly sufficient proof of sustained and constructive thinking. Rabindra Nath is a very great poet, but not really a very sound thinker, though mistaken for one by people for many years. He is a mighty creator of ideals, but not really a capable builder of systems. His soul is an exquisitely sensitive instrument for catching the most subtle emotional impulses or spiritual inspirations about him. And like all sensitive instruments, it is extremely liable to outer influences. His environments have, therefore, always influenced him far more powerfully than what one sees usually in the case of more masculine spirits. But like all creators, Rabindra Nath too, while being profoundly influenced by his surroundings, yet by his very response to these, lends a meaning and inspiration to them which they never had before. It happened in the history of his connection with the new nationalist movement in Bengal. Rabindra Nath's nationalism was not the fruit of his thought, but only a lofty and overwhelming impulse of his emotions. It was not speculative, in the highest sense of the term, based upon any broad generalisation of social experience or political philosophy; but was simply intuitive, the creation of his supersensitive spirit, wounded by the cruel actualities of the conflicts between Indian and British interests in the present political, economic, and even social and intellectual life of his people. The partition of Bengal, carried out in the face of the United protests and supplications of the Bengalee people, wounded his national self-respect, and under the impulse of that emotion he came out of his comparative retirement, to take his place in the very forefront of the leaders of the anti-partition agitation. The idea of the Rakhi Celebrations, first inaugurated on the 16th of October, 1905, the day when the partition was formally effected, as a standing protest against the official attempt to divide the Bengalee race, originated with Rabindra Nath. It was he who had first preached the duty of eschewing all voluntary associations with official activities, and of applying ourselves to the organisation of our economic, social, and educational life, independently of official help and control. Though the Boycott of British Goods, as a protest against the partition of Bengal, originated with others, and was adopted by the political leaders of the country, in public meeting assembled, in the Town Hall of Calcutta, it was Rabindra Nath who first propounded an elaborate scheme for the practical boycott of the administration to the farthest limits that the laws of the land allow us to do so. Though the idea of a National University did not exactly originate with Rabindra Nath, he was the first to propose a boycott of the examinations of the Calcutta University, in 1906, and, thereby, to push the scheme of national education towards practical realisation. By all these things, Rabindra Nath, whether consciously or unconsciously, had created for himself a unique position in the thoughts and activities of the new nationalist movement in his province. All these were, however, more or less the passing impulses of the sensitive-poets, and not the considered resolves of the far-seeing statesman. Rabindra Nath himself like many others of infinitely lower powers and lesser note, simply caught the soul-stirring inspiration of this new nationalism, but did not grasp the fundamental, social and political philosophy which lay at its back. Indeed, while his poetic inspiration is divinely superb, his social philosophy has always been painfully crude. One recognised this crude social philosophy in his essays on "Indian History" and "Brahman," read at public meetings, in the Metropolitan Institution Hall, in the summer of 1902 or '3. The same limitations marked his scheme of the Swadeshi Samaj propounded before the partition of Bengal, though kept alive for some time even after the anti-partition agitation had started. There was neither any systematic thinking nor even any really constructive imagination, which is the soul of high statesmanship, behind these creations of Rabindra Nath. They were only fine products of his poetic fancy. Consequently they could not stand the test of the cruel actualities of the exceedingly tense and nervous situation which followed the first outburst of this nationalist upheaval in Bengal. These actualities drove Rabindra Nath from his old emotional nationalism into a new cosmopolitanism or universalism, which was not the logical perfection and fulfilment of nationalism, but practically its denial and antithesis. Had Rabindra Nath a full grasp of the true philosophy of nationalism, he would have tried to correct the excesses of those who were drifting swiftly from nationalism into revolutionary anarchism, under the inspiration of alien ideas and examples,—not by practically repudiating the supreme truth and value of nationalism itself, but by presenting these in their true light and correct perspective, as necessary moments and permanent vehicles of the progressive life of universal humanity. Nationalism as a mere political cry or principle, which embodies only the desire for the isolated independence and self-assertion of different national units, and inspires their ambition for the exploitation of, or domination over, other weaker nationalities, has little or no moral message for the world. But as the desire and the demand of the individuality of different nations, as embodied in their special and specific culture and character, to freely and fully develop itself with a view to make its special contributions to the common life or universal humanity,—this nationalism is a thing of the highest moral and spiritual significance to the race. It is a secret, as the human personality and its right of free movement for its own realisation, within the limits which the similar right of other nationalities impose upon it, is as much a divine thing, ordained for the highest moral elevation of the race, as individual human freedom itself. As individual freedom make for the advancement and uplift of human society, even so national autonomy makes for the general progress and evolution of universal humanity. As every social organism expresses and realises its highest life in and through the perfection of the lives of the individuals composing it, even so does this universal Humanity express and realise itself in and through the lives of different individual nationalities. As the collective life and end of each Society is not an abstraction but a reality though not apart from, but only in and through, the special and particular lives and ends of its individual members, even so the collective life of this Universal Humanity too is not a mere abstraction, like blackness or goodness, for instance, which exists only as a mode of our thought, and is found nowhere in actual objective experience,—but is a reality, though that reality is not something apart from, but organically bound up with, the actual life and evolution of different nationalities. The universal is not something which exists by destroying the particularities of the particulars but which rather completes and fulfils them. The universal which ignores or negates the particular is not the true universal, but only what is called an abstract universal. Universal Humanity, which ignores or negates the nationality, is a mere abstraction, which may lend itself to the building of airy fairy fancies, but cannot lend truth and vitality to the actual work of human fellowship and social progress. Least of all can it help the settlement of the crude conflicts of half-truths of which most of the struggles, Rabindra Nath however sought refuge in the fanciful peace of an abstract universalism or cosmopolitanism. This is the form that his re-action against the lawless excesses of certain aspects of the new nationalist upheaval in Bengal, rapidly assumed ; and it gradually drifted him away from the central currents of that great movement of which he had been one of the earliest, and by far the most, powerful and inspiring leader.

Henceforward, Rabindra Nath seems to have been almost completely absessed by this abstract universalism, which has marked unmistakably all his later pronouncements, whether theological, or ethical, or social. Though born in the Brahmo Samaj, Rabindra Nath had never before evinced any strong partiality for the abstractions of popular Brahmo theology or ethics, or had openly identified himself with the sanctimonious and sectarian militancy of the Brahmo Propaganda. As a protestant and reform movement, the Brahmo Samaj, naturally, lays stronger and more frequent emphasis upon the errors and evils of Hindu thought and institutions than upon their truth or good. Rabindra Nath had never before openly taken up the role of either the social or the religious reformer. His patriotism was too sensitive, and his sympathies too broad, to fit in with the mental and moral requirements of this office. The violent re-action against the excesses of revolutionary nationalism rapidly drove him however to seek a safe and sympathetic field of activity in the propaganda of Brahmo Samaj. Here again he could not shape his environments to his own superior institutions and refined sensibilities, but succumbed practically to their influences and thus created a new cleavage between himself and his old following in the country who counted immensely more Hindus than Brahmos. This cleavage became somewhat painfully prominent on the eve of his departure for Europe. Unfriendly critics did not even hesitate to say that his literary work was practically finished, and his usefulness exhausted, and that he must henceforth live only upon the reputation of his past achievements.

Rabindra Nath's unique popularity among his educated countrymen, was, thus, falling somewhat under a cloud when he sailed for Europe. Of course it did not affect his position as the greatest of modern Bengalee poets. But Rabindra Nath was something more than a poet. He was also a great thought leader. And it was his position as a leader of the thought-life of his people, which was visibly losing ground, when he started upon his last pilgrimage to England. People did not understand the meaning of his pilgrimage. He did not take them into his confidence. It is very likely that he himself had no clear idea about it. It was a mysterious call, an overwhelming impulse, which so often conceals the purposes of Providence in our lives, that evidently drove him there. And it was only when he saw a wide field of public usefulness opening out to him, through his new friendships in London and elsewhere, that their true inwardness of his call to Europe was clearly revealed to him. And he must have at once seen in this a most wonderful province of the fulfilment of his latest mission in life.

That mission was, unmistakably, one of atonement and reconciliation. Ever since the manifestations of revolutionary tendencies in Bengal, Rabindra Nath had commenced to increasingly realise the supreme moral and spiritual significance of England's presence in India. Others had also seen and proclaimed the moral meaning of British Rule; it is true. It was, indeed, a common article of faith with all our social and religious reformers of the Victorian era. Some of them, perhaps, hold the same view even to-day. It has also been a notorious cant among Anglo-Indian Administrators and British

Politicians. Rabindra Nath, however, did not understand it in the old sense. The old view had presented England as the moral and spiritual regenerator of India. It practically sought to add moral and intellectual bondage to our outer political subjection to England. It wanted, whether consciously or unconsciously, our political fealty to the British Government in India to be deepened and strengthened by our moral and intellectual allegiance to British thoughts and ideals. Rabindra Nath could never, and did not, revive this old view, which he had himself so powerfully attacked and exposed. The moral purpose of the British connection was revealed to him not in the old but in an altogether new light and meaning. Rabindra Nath stood out here not as a successor of Keshub Chander Sen, but rather as an inheritor of Swami Vivekanand. To Rabindra Nath, England not only had a mission in India; but India herself had a supreme spiritual message for England and Europe. There are many things that India has learnt and will learn from England and Europe; but there are as many things, if not more, that England

and Europe must equally learn from India. England by the very strength and rudeness of her attack upon Indian life and thought, had aroused that ancient land from her age-long stupor; and so far she has undoubtedly been a regenerator of India. But the highest fulfilment of this new awakening will come only when India is able to lend the help of her accumulated experience, and illumination of her philosophy, and the inspiration of her vision of the universal, to her regenerator, and, through her, to others who share with her both the glories and the tribulations of their common culture and civilisation. This is the superme moral purpose in modern Indian History which Rabindra Nath has been increasingly recognising of late years. This is both the cause and the effect of his repulsion towards the revolutionary excesses of certain sections of the Bengalee nationalists. It was the key-note of most of his public utterances in 1908 and 09 and 10. It was perhaps present in his subliminal consciousness all along. Nothing that he has said or done before, really, contradicts this view. To fulfil the moral end of modern Indian history and evolution, it was absolutely necessary that the spell which the European illumination had cast over educated India should be broken. And Rabindra Nath worked perhaps more than any of his compatriots to break this spell. It was essential that, to pursue her mission among modern peoples, India should be thoroughly conscious of her own self. And no one among us has helped this quickening more than Rabindra Nath. A revolt against the intellectual and moral bondage of European civilisation was absolutely necessary for the fulfilment of this mission. And Rabindra Nath has led this revolt with greater courage and effect than any one else. He has thus taken his share of all this arduous and unpleasant work. But all these are mere preliminaries. The real fulfilment of this mission must be sought and found, however, not in mere revolt, but in that closer reconciliation which is the only ethical end and justification of all revolts. The high ends of this mission will not be served by the perpetuation of racial conflicts, but only in and through that final settlement and synthesis which is the

Logical and Ethical objective of all conflicts. The powerful pen of Rabindra Nath had, for some time previous to his departure for Europe, been almost entirely consecrated to the cause of this reconciliation and atonement. Unfortunately, however, even as the inspiration of his earlier revolt had come not primarily from his intellect, but only from his emotions, so the inspiration of this new gospel of peace and reconciliation also came from the same ethereal source. The appeal was not to the intellect but to the emotions only. And as long as the intellect remained unconvinced of the reality of this peace or the possibility of this reconciliation, the heart refused, necessarily, to respond to the fairy creations of the poet's fancy. His appeal, therefore, fell absolutely flat upon people overwhelmed with the bearing down sense of the cruel actuality of their life and struggles. But the very causes that led to the failure of Rabindra Nath's latest mission among his own people, contributed very materially, I think, to its wonderful success in England.

Rabindra Nath as a nationalist poet

and leader would have found almost every door shut against him in England. Few people in this country have any idea of the immense influence that the retired Anglo-Indian community of London exercise over the India Office and its environments. And no Indian can now get a hearing from the leaders of English life and thought, unless the India Office stands sponsor to his work, either directly or indirectly. The airy abstractions of Rabindra Nath's latter-day Cosmopolitanism, while they failed absolutely to catch the popular imagination in India, however considerably rehabilitated him among Anglo Indian Officials. And once official prejudice was broken down in India, it was not very difficult to secure official patronage in England. Rabindra Nath was very fortunate in receiving the recognition of the India Office, indirect though it was; for without it, he could never have received that free appreciation from the English press which has been mainly instrumental in securing for him this year's Nobel Prize for literature.

But however helpful the sympathy

and support of the India Office may have been to Rabindra Nath's recent work in England, it was at best only a mere negative character. It simply moved all likely prejudices against him as a nationalist leader of Bengal, but did not create his high poetic genius, which, once all physical obstacles were removed from its way, captured the British mind by the force of its own intrinsic beauty and worth. No man can convert the crow into a cuckoo; and no official sympathy or support could have ever secured for any lesser man than Rabindra Nath the high recognition that he has received from the British public. In seeking to form, however, correct estimate, not of Rabindra Nath's genius, but only of this European recognition, these extraneous causes and conditions should neither be ignored nor mis-judged. It is because that these have not so far received due consideration from our people, that the congratulations to Rabindra Nath upon his selection for the Nobel Prize for Literature, have been almost uniformly marked by an utter lack of the sense of proportion. And in considering these extraneous causes, we must frankly realise it, that while many things have brought about this Nobel Award, not the least important among these has been the political move of the Anglo-Indian community, and particularly of the India Office in London. The times were indeed, very favourable for this English work of Rabindra Nath. He was called there at just the right psychological moment. Science with its excessive emphasis on so-called facts, had commenced to painfully starve the imagination of European humanity, and art under the tyranny of its own technique, had well nigh killed the native freedom of their fancy. This vain attempt of the senses to conquer the supersensuous, and of forms to overwhelm the spirit or the idea, threatened to carry European art back from neo-romanticism to what may be best described as neo-orientalism, in the Hegelian sense. All this carnival of the senses had, however, commenced to create a natural revulsion in the European mind. The sensuous did not fully meet the inner idealities of the modern consciousness on the one hand, while on the other, it had not found back its lost faith in the supersensuous. The conflict between matter and spirit, between the seen and the unseen, between signs with its demands for definition, and philosophy with its intuitions of the infinite, was keen, and seemed hopeless of settlement. Mediæval thought in Europe had tried to overcome this eternal conflict by practically denying all positive moral values to the sensuous and the material, and placing the world, the flesh and the devil, all in one and the same category; and had sought to build up the higher life of humanity upon a system of logical abstractions, overwhelming the natural life of man by supernatural faiths and fears. The Renaissance, while it killed the influence of these mediæval abstraction, helped however to practically paganise modern culture. This culture, with its excessive emphasis on definition, its keen sense of form, and its superb perceptions of beauty, looks, indeed, from some points of view very much like a revived Greek culture. Ibsen who was the idol of fashionable society a quarter of a century ago; Neitzsche, who is regarded as the prophet of a new era, with his gospel of the superman, in many quarters to-day are both essentially Pagans. Bernard Shaw would, perhaps, not care to disclaim the distinction. But not only in Literature and Art, but equally in moral and religion as well, one cannot fail to recognise this pagan influence in modern era. The ethical inspiration of modern Eugenica, with its Crusade against the physically or mentally weak or unfit, and its practical demand for their complete elimination from the course of racial evolution, is not Christian but Greek; while the dominant note of Divine immanence in Modern Theology, with its feebler hold on both the transcendence and the personality of God, cannot entirely disclaim this overwhelming pagan influence and inspiration. This new conflict between popular and traditional Christian faiths and ideals, and the revived spirit of paganism is the most notable feature of contemporary thought and life in Europe. It has completely unsettled people's mind. Those who, at one time, had rushed with wild enthusiasm out of their old Christian bondage, into the new freedom of this pagan revival, have commenced to find out the insufficiency of the new thoughts and ideals to fully satisfy the demands of their reason or the cravings of their emotions. On the other hand, they find it impossible to go back to the mental abstractions of Christian Theology or the forensic conflicts of Christian ethics. The pagan Renaissance has completely exhausted itself, in working up the present revolt and antethesis in European thought; it has no message of reconciliation and synthesis. But Europe is hankering for some higher synthesis, which will reconcile the seen with the unseen, the sensuous with the super-sensuous, the material with the spiritual, the natural with the moral, the apparent with the evils of life with the ideal of real good. The world, the flesh, and the devil are too lovely to be thrown away, too real to be negated, too strong to be completely overcome. They have been with man ever since man became man, and though treated as an enemy and sought to be destroyed by him, through countless generation, they are yet as lively as ever. And since they cannot be conquered, they must be conciliated.

This is the demand of the modern consciousness. There must be a settlement of this endless dispute. And England saw, evidently, some glimpses, however felt, of the promise of this reconciliation in Rabindra Nath's message. This is the inner psychology of the success of his latest mission in Europe.

Few, indeed, if any, of Rabindra Nath's Bengalee admirers would place his Bengalee Gitanjalee among the best of his productions. To my mind, Rabindra Nath has given us his best and highest in his Urbhashi, and Chitrangada his Patita, and other lyrics which appear under the heading of "Woman" in his collected works. By some competent critics, Sonar Taree is, I know, adjudged as the most superb of his creations. There are numerous other pieces also, scattered over different sections of these collections, which would equally establish his claims to the very foremost ranks of modern poets, in India or Europe. But his GITANJALEE does not come near to any of these. These are the outpourings of his religious intuitions. And, as such, they lack that clarity of inner vision and that firm grasp of spiritual reality, with which his Bengalee readers are familiar in their old poets. The human and the divine boldly intermingle with one another, in the religious poetry of Bengal. They are as intensely real as they are spiritual, as solidly human as they are divine. This is equally true of both our Vaishnava and our Shakta poets. Both Vaishnavism with its complete grasp of the concrete Universal or Saguna Brahman, and Shaktism with its equally complete hold upon the universe form of the Absolute, lend themselves to the creation of realistic representations of the deepest spiritual experiences, which neither Hebrew or Protestant Christian theism can possibly do. And Rabindra Nath's theism is more closely arrived to Hebrew and Unitarian Christian theism, which is really the inevitable logic of Protestant Christianity, than to true Hindu theism, the highest expression of which is found in our Vaishnava and Shaiva Schools. But the very abstractions of Rabindra Nath's religious pieces, their very impalpableness, so to say, which failed to touch the deeper cause of the heart of the Bengalee people, fed for generation upon the concrete idealism of their Vaishnava and Shakta poets, had, however, a strange fascination for men and women whose jaded spirits had already commenced to turn away from the crude realism of Modern Europe. The half sensuous and half supersensuous fancies of the GITANJALEE, which are human without being carnal and spiritual without being unnatural, which by their very simplicity and incoherence, lend themselves equally to realistic and human as to spiritualistic and divine interpretations, have appealed with great force to people groping after the unseen and the spiritual. Here they found a God without Theology, a religion without ritual, a spirituality without superstition, the vague fragrance of an idealism which neither cruelly repudiated nor shamefacedly embraced, the solid sensualities of life. Above all here was the charm of " Oriental " manners, and " Eastern " imageries, for which Europe had commenced to develope a new test. Here was something out of the way, something fresh and strange, something unexplored and ununderstood. And all these things contributed to create the great popularity that the GITANJALEE has attained in England and Europe.

But however may be the intrinsic merits of the English GITANJALEE, considered either by itself or in relation to the others superior creations of its own author, that it marks a new movement in modern world-thought cannot be denied. For many years past an international fraternisation has been in progress closer than any that had been known before among the various vernacular literatures of Europe. But this is the first time that a non-European vernacular has found admission into this fraternity. The award of the Nobel Prize will lead to the translation of this English GITANJALEE into the other European vernaculars, and will gradually open out the way to the production of similar translations, not only of the other works of Rabindra Nath himself, but also of other Bengalee writers both ancient and modern; and by this means the Literature of Bengal, and by and by the other Indian Vernacular literatures also will be introduced into this international fraternity. This is the supreme significance and the highest work of this Novel Award. As a recognition of Rabindra Nath's high poetic genius, it can have no real worth to his own people, and hardly even to himself. As an opening for Bengalee thought and culture as a contributory force in modern world-thought and Universal human culture, its supreme value cannot be denied, but should be gratefully acknowledged. Even those of his people, who could not whole heartedly follow Rabindra Nath in his later evolutions, should frankly recognise in this new promise of usefulness for their thought and culture in the larger life of modern humanity an ample compensation for their own loss.

From some points of view it may, indeed be very justly held that by his latest English visit, Rabindra Nath has rendered a much greater service to his Country and his times than what any other Bengalee had done, whether dead or living. He has opened the way for a real fellowship between India and Europe and particularly between India and England wherein history must seek and find the only moral justification for the present British connection. This connection has been like all earthly things a mixture of both good and evil. Both parties have gained something through this connection, and when the accounts are carefully made up, the particular gains on either side may not be found to fully balance their respective losses. But the Providence who presides over the destinies of Nations and shapes the course of their historic evolution, pays precious little heed to these petty particularities of their gains and losses. He works only and always for universal ends. His justice is larger than, and is even different from, what we call and claim as such in our selfish conflicts with one another. The individual suffers, but the world is more and more:—that is His Justice. For that is the final and absolute justification of all the apparent evils that large and world-referring historic movements inflict upon particular nations our communities. And that the world will be the gainer through the present connection between India and England, has been brought home to us more clearly than before, by the success of Rabindra Nath's

English work. Others had gone to England upon the same mission, it is true. Ram Mohan Roy, Keshub Chander Sen, Vivekanand, had all worked for the same end. But none of them had been able to achieve what Rabindranath had done. Ram Mohan Roy and Keshub Chander Sen gained high recognition for their personal culture and character, from the British people, but hardly raised their race and civilization in the estimation of the Britisher to the extent that Rabindranath has done. Ram Mohan Roy's message was, no doubt, the message of higher Hindu thought and culture; but it fell, practically upon barren ground. What the leaders of English thought and society saw in the Raja was a man of very high intellectual endowments and equipments, but these were hardly recognised as having any special reference to the culture and civilisation of his race. Keshub Chander Sen, in his English visit, proved more the capacity of Indians to assimilate European culture, than their claims to broaden and deepen it, by original contributions. Vivekanad was the first Indian who boldly asserted these claims. His was the first genuine Hindu message to Europe and America. But the effect of Vivekananda's American Mission was more visibly and widely felt in India itself than in Europe or America. It quickened our self-conscientiousness far more than it was able to establish any real and abiding intellectual and moral relations between India and Christendom. It was, indeed impossible in the very nature of things. Vivekananda's was an intellectual mission. He went to preach certain doctrines, to promulgate a particular theology and to convert people into his views. It was, therefore, necessarily a message of War, and not of peace. It was a mission of conversion, which involved conflict. Though, therefore, Vivekanand aroused profound enthusiasm amongst a limited circle in both England and America, people at large either ignored him altogether or opposed him vehemently. But Rabindranath's appeal is not to their intellect but to their emotions. He has preached no doctrine, promulgated no dogmas, made no attack upon popular faiths and beliefs. He had not hurt their conceit, nor upset their self-complacence. He has not disturbed their faiths, nor sought to revolutionise their life. He has not tried to break idols. He has done nothing in short, to set people's back up against him. He has simply sought to please them. His appeal has been to their sense of the beautiful. It has been an appeal to their starved spirits and their thirsting heart. He has showed a way—the only way that they could understand—of reconciling their present intellectual and moral conflicts, and has prescribed a remedy—the only remedy that was suited to their condition and constitution—for their troubled and wearied spirits. He has, therefore, won, where Vivekanand failed. He has opened a highway for the interchange of intellectual and moral commodities between India and England.

This is, to my mind, the fairest and most correct estimate of Rabindranath's latest work in Europe. That work is both intensely national and broadly humanitarian. This is what Rabindranath was evidently called to do in England. The Nobel Prize with all that it means intellectually and morally, is the fullest justification of his last pilgrimage to the West. He had expected a frank recognition of this fact from his people. But while they indulged in all sorts of wild exaggerations in offering him their congratulations upon the Nobel Award, they completely overlooked the one thing that made it significant to Rabindranath himself. This is what must have caused all that irritation which found such candid expression in his reply to the address of the Bolepur Deputaion. And this is what fully justified the rebuke that they got from him, apparently inhospitable though it was.

SIR TARAK NATH PALIT

Man is a curious bundle of contradictions, and the more real a man is, the greater and more perplexing seem to be the contradictions of his life and conduct. In fact, the man who is not a contradiction, can hardly be called a character. Mr. Tarak Nath Palit, recently knighted in recognition of his munificent gift to the Calcutta University, is, by common consent, a character. He has, therefore, stood somewhat, out of the common run of his contemporaries, among the English educated community of Bengal. One of the ablest members of the Calcutta Bar, Mr. Palit did not earn the distinction that fell to the lot of many of his brother-Barristers, not because he had not their ability or even their opportunity, but because he had a sturdy independence, which was sometimes interpreted by some people even as a vicious temper, and that is a thing which never pays in any profession, not even in the so-called independent profession of law. He never put up with any nonsense, neither from Judge nor from counsel, and least of all from the Anglo-Indian Judge or the English Counsel. And no counsel, however able he might be, has any chance of getting to the top of his profession, unless he can stand well in the good grace of the Court. Tarak Nath Palit never tried to do so. He never would have succeeded even if he had tried it. And this is why, despite his very superior endowments and acquirements, he did not gain the distinction that some of our Bengaiee Barristers did in his time.

The same reasons worked to keep him more or less out of our political platform and public life also. The man who would not play up to the Judges of the High Court, could not be expected to play down to the gallery in our Congresses and Conferences. Compromise is the very soul of public life. In the true statesman, the spirit of compromise is a very high quality. There its end is to avoid or minimise the possibilities of coming evils and secure and advance those of future good. In the petty politician, expediency is whose one universal principle of life, this compromise is a mean and degrading thing, calculated to demoralise rather than to uplift personal character or public life. This compromise had no place in the philosophy of Tarak Nath Palit. He could never stoop, not even to conquer. He knew many of the men who were running our public political shows. He knew from behind the scene the amount of paint and powder that goes usually to the make-up of the ordinary patriot and politician in this country ; and, therefore, not having the suavity that could be all things unto all men, he never made the vain attempt of playing this role. This is why he is not so widely known in other parts of India as some of our old Barristers have been. Even in his own Province, Tarak Nath Palit never was a force in its public life. And no one ever dreamt that he would, in the evening of his days, secure for himself a lasting place in the gratitude of his people, by dedicating the entire savings of a life-time, to the cause of scientific education in his country. This is practically the one public act of his ; and it has, to a very large extent, revolutionised all the popular estimates of the man.

Yet, if one had critically analysed his character, one would have easily seen that Tarak Nath Palit's is that type of personality which is most capable of making the greatest sacrifice if only the object which demanded it could touch his heart. Inside a very rough and even repellent exterior, Tarak Nath has been known, from his boyhood, to carry a very tender and highly susceptible heart. Like many a greater man, he has a brusque manner, a terrible tongue and a quick temper, joined to a very impulsive and not ungenerous disposition. He has, therefore, been known to be most steadfast of friends and the most relentless of foes in private life. No one could do the least evil turn to any of Tarak Nath Palit's friends, without making him an enemy for life. Certain aspects of Sir Tarak Nath Palit's character reminds one sometimes of Pandit Ishwar Chandra Vidyasagar. Of course, there is very wide difference between the two men. But this difference is more quantitative than qualitative. The same sturdy independence, the same quick temper and brusque manners, joined to a soft and susceptible heart, characterise Tarak Nath Palit as did the great Bengalee Philanthrophist. And there is also the same assumption of cynicism in his as was characteristic of Vidya Sagar. Tarak Nath Palit has also the keen humour which one always found in Pandit Ishwar Chander. And lastly, by his great gift, Sir Tarak Nath has secured for himself a place, though much smaller and lower, in the same niche in the history of modern education in Bengal, where the memory of Pandit Ishwar Chunder Vidyasagar is lovingly enshrined.

Tarak Nath Palit has not been a saint, and it would be doing him great injustice to try to canonise him now for his great gift to the Calcutta University. Saints don't grow, as the late Lord Salisbury once said at the banquet of the Royal Academy in London, in modern civilisation; and to paint the modern man or woman as a saint would be, his Lordship reminded us, to risk prosecution for libel in our law courts.

Nor is there any need to take that

risk in Sir Tarak Nath's case. For he would be the last person to appreciate such pleasant exaggerations. For whatever his faults, Sir Tarak Nath has never been a humbug in all his life. A nature like his could not, in fact, play the part. And it is for this reason that even those who do not like him, cannot refuse to respect him.

But for all that, Sir Tarak Nath's offer to endow a Technical College in connection with the National Council of Education, Bengal, was received with considerable distrust by a large section of his educated countrymen. He had never posed as a patriot or Philanthropist before. And owing to his want of confidence in the current public life of his country, he could not feel sure that his gift would, if absolutely made over to the National Council, secure reasonable permanence to the Institution that he wanted to establish. This is why he was cautious, and as it seemed to some, even vacillating in his dealings with that body. We did not like Sir Tarak Nath's attitude in this matter at the time. As he was suspicious of the Council, so a large section of his countrymen were equally suspicious of him. He did not believe in the capacity of the National Council; and many people did not believe in the sincerity of Sir Tarak Nath. Events have, however, proved, I think, that he was right and we were wrong. For it can scarcely be denied that the National Council has not been faithful to its charge. The movement that called the Council into existence is dead. The Institution that sought to concretise the ideal of National Education among us, lies almost still-born. An experienced man of affairs, Sir Tarak Nath evidently presaged it all: and so he did not like to throw away so much good money upon a wild goose-chase. It is a pity that the National Council could not get the trusteeship of this large fund: but it is not so much the fault of the donor as of the Council itself. He might have placed his donation with the Calcutta University seven years ago; if he did not do it, it was because he was sincerely anxious to have it administered by a people's organisation. And it is only the failure of the Bengal National Council to justify itself that has led to the final disposition of the money to the Calcutta University. And one cannot justly hold that Sir Tarak has not done right in this matter.

And the conditions of the gift show that Sir Tarak Nath has tried his best to preserve as much as possible the original idea of his endowment. All the Professors connected with it will have to be Indians. I have been told that there was considerable difficulty in getting the Government and University accept his gift on this condition. Theoretically it does seem rather invidious to make any such condition in regard to the working of an education institution whose one end should be to secure the best training for those who may be placed in it. But under present conditions, when the Indian Educational service, as reconstituted by Lord Curzon, offers such restricted opportunities to Indian talents, the imposition of some such racial limitation in the working of the new endowment was absolutely necessary. Without this condition, Sir Tarak Nath's munificent gift would have practically failed of its real purpose, namely, the promotion of scientific culture among his people. But I have very grave doubts whether Sir Tarak Nath would have got this condition accepted by the University,.if the (then) present Vice-Chancellor, Sir Ashutosh Mukherjee, had not used all his subtle influence with the authorities in favour of the offer.

BAL GANGADHAR TILAK

MR. TILAK'S RELEASE

Every Indian Nationalist must have received with sincere gratitude the news of Mr. Tilak's release, and particularly, the announcement that, on the whole, his health has not been materially affected by the trials that have been heaped upon him, during the past six years and more. I have no desire to rake up the past, at this moment, or review the circumstances that led to his trial, conviction, and punishment. Sufficient be it for his friends to know that he was treated with every possible kindness and consideration during his long incarceration, and has been able to build up more than the super-structure of two or three volumes of scholarly and inspiring work dealing with the ideals and culture of his race. Let us seek and find in these whatever compensations Providence has provided for all his troubles and privations, and the pain and sorrow of his numerous friends and admirers in this country. Indeed, it seems to me, that, after all, by the way he has been able to utilise this long period of enforced rest and isolation Mr. Tilak has proved himself a much greater and mightier man than even what he had been known to be. He clearly took his position with absolute trust in that Power which shapes men's lives to His own inscrutable ends. He has thus proved his title to something far higher and greater than the honour of mere political leadership or statesmanly wisdom. Here one sees in him not merely the intrepid politician and selfless patriot, but something, indeed, of the stuff of which the saints and seers of the race are made. We always knew that all this was there, but the world had not received any ocular proof of it as yet. And by quietly and unconsciously furnishing this proof of a new and superior moral heroism and spiritual strength, Bal Gangadhar Tilak stands to-day in the love and admiration of his countrymen, upon a much higher pedestal than what he had occupied before. May he be spared long to his country and his people !

Mr. TILAK'S POLITICS

Even as a mere politician, Mr. Tilak while always moved by a lofty and passionate idealism, never lost hold of the solid actualities about him. Indian politicians may be broadly divided into two classes, those that are masters of the small details of practical administrative needs and tendencies, and are therefore, engaged in shaping and controlling these towards the broader channels of our national life; and those who are moved by a vision of these ultimate ideas and ideals, and are trying to build up the mental and moral super-structure upon which these must be set up and concretised. Some are idealists, and some are practical workers. In Mr. Tilak we have always found a splendid combination of the vision of the idealist, with the practical wisdom of the experienced man of affairs. This has, perhaps, been his great misfortune personally. A mere practical politician, he could have safely served his country along such lines as have secured to Mr. Gopal Krishna Gokhale, his unique position in current Indian politics. A mere idealist, Mr. Tilak considering his broad scholarship, superior intellect, rare self-possession, and capacity for absolute disattachment from the fleeting eternals of life, could have easily remained a dreamer of noble dreams, inspiring the populace to devoted and selfless service in the cause of their country, but himself but little mixed up with their activities, and, therefore more or less safe from the trials and tribulations that dog the steps of the religious, social or political reformer. But he was neither an accommodating politician working only for immediate ends, nor a dreaming idealist, endowed with the magic power of negating the real, in the pursuit of the ideal; but a strange combination of the two; he, therefore, missed the advantages of either and reaped the troubles of both. Still greater has been, I think, his misfortune, in being a leader of his people in Bombay. No one who has any inside knowledge of the public life of Bombay, can cherish much respect for it. Public life in Bengal may, and perhaps really does, lack the practical wisdom of Bombay, which means in plain English, the habit of lightly treading the tortuous paths of diplomacy; but it is, at any rate, much more frank and open, and for that very reason, much purer than that of Bombay, with her mixed inheritance in her historic past, and her capacity for endless intrigue, which marked both the rise and the fall of the Mahratta Confederacy—such as the peculiar situation of the days of Moghal decadence naturally called forth. All these are absent in Bengal which has no living historical memories of the immediate past. This is our one great peculiarity. It is, I think, a full and satisfactory compensation that Providence has provided for us for our lack of living historic antecedents. Had Mr. Tilak been a Bengalee, he would never have been called upon to suffer all that he has had to suffer. On the other hand, I know of no Bengalee leader, Moderate or Extremist, who could have so heroically borne all these trials and tribulations, as he has done. Taken all in all, it must, I think, be admitted, that Mr. Balgangadhar Tilak is a unique character in our modern public life, so strong yet so quiet, so practical yet so idealistic, with such great devotion or bhakti and yet so little religiosity, at once so conservative yet so broad-visioned, with such grasp of the ultimate ideal ends and, at the same time, such a mastery of the details of immediate actualities. The like of him I have never found in my more or less intimate acquaintance of the last forty years of Indian public life.

* * * *

UNFORTUNATE MISUNDERSTANDINGS

It was almost inevitable that so complex a character and personality as this, should have been so wofully misunderstood by both friends and foes alike. And no one seems to have misunderstood this great Mahratta Brahman more than the Bombay Bureaucracy. They failed from the very beginning to understand it that if there was any one in Bombay who could help a rational and effective solution of the complex and anxious problems of Indian politics, Mr. Tilak was that man. He knew the soul of his people. He knew both the strength and the weakness of his fellow countrymen. He knew completely what they had and what they lacked. This knowledge could not be claimed by either the Indian politician about the courts and palaces of the Government, nor by the rulers themselves. He was, I think, the first educated Indian who realised that our public life must be brought into direct and living touch with the silent life and ideals, institutions and pageants, of the masses, if it was to be a driving force in modern Indian history and evolution. While, therefore, others were engaged in agitating for popular rights, Mr. Tilak applied himself to educating the populace, along their own familiar lines, through the plastic ceremonials and rituals of their traditional religion. His profitable excursions into the realm of ancient Sanskrit literature, had revealed to him the truth, so frequently ignored or missed, not only by foreign but even by Indian scholars themselves, that the sacraments and ceremonials of popular and Pauranic Hinduism had always a supreme socio-ethical reference. These are not mere religious institutions, as religious institutions are understood in Christendom, but powerful vehicles of the social, and even the civic, life of the masses. This is how, it seems to me he received the inspiration of reviving the Ganapati-pujas and use them, as of old, as a vehicle for the quickening of national life and ambition in the Hindu populace of the Deccan. English education and far more than English education, the methods of British Administration, had breathed a new life into the dry bones of India. Signs of a religious and social revolt were evident on all sides. The question was how to shape these new forces, so that they might realise their own ends with the least little possible disturbance of the existing order. If we failed to attach the new life to the ancient traditions of the country, the new wine would be too strong for the old life, and a revolution similar to those that have marked the course of progress and civilisation in modern Europe, would inevitably burst over this peaceful land, and the violence of it would be in direct ratio to the peace and stupor that preceded it. Had the Bombay official mind any clear grasp of the real psychology of the situation that faced them, and which Mr. Tilak was seeking to solve in this way, they would have sought to treat him as a friend and tried to remove any possibilities of mischief that they might have feared from him, not by persecuting or prosecuting him as an enemy or a rebel, but associating themselves as far as possible, with his propaganda. They did not or could not see the wisdom of this course. They did condescend to take a full measure of the possibilities not only of the man, but of the movement that he had inaugurated. They commenced to keep him at arm's length. They could not or would not see that there was one man at least who worked for his country with absolute singleness of mind, who had no personal ambitions and who would, therefore, be no more be tempted by office or honour than cowed down by threats or prosecutions. People do not generally realise it that the opponent who cannot be bought, can, if possible, be crushed, but can never be cowed down. A frank and friendly alliance upon the basis of a rational reconciliation of apparently opposing interests is the only course that wisdom prompts in all dealings with these pure and selfless men. It is exceedingly unfortunate that the authorities in Bombay did not see the wisdom of this course; or both the Government and the people would have been saved a lot of trouble and anxiety that they have to pass during all these years.

MR. TILAK'S NATIONALISM

Mr. Bal Gangadhar Tilak may have opposed, in the course of his duties as a journalist and politician, the bureaucracy in Bombay and the manner of his criticism of their acts and policy may have wounded official susceptibilities; but it is not, I think, at all just to accuse him of any criminal or revolutionary aims. He was, even in the exciting days of the Swadeshi agitation, at the most a passive resister, who set a much narrower limit to his propaganda of passive resistance than what Mr. Gandhi openly and admittedly did in South Africa. It need not be ignored or denied that the passive resistance movement, though absolutely lawful and unexceptionable in theory, lends itself almost inevitably to lawless excesses in a country like India, so extensive in area and so diverse in regard to its populations, and where, therefore, it is absolutely impossible to find that effective leadership and that concerted action, which was possible in a small community like that of the Indians in South Africa. What is safe in Africa, under the peculiar conditions of that country, could not be safe here in India. There is no harm in frankly confessing it that the Nationalist leaders in India, like Mr. Tilak and others, did not fully realise the impossibility of exercising an effective control over their following, particularly in view of the stern attitude assumed towards the whole movement with which they were associated, by the executive authorities all over India. One may very reasonably surmise that even the Congress leaders would have found it impossible to control and direct the outburst of enthusiasm with which the earlier sessions of the Congress had been associated, if the Government had not almost openly encouraged it at first, and even when this patronage was withdrawn, if they had not benevolently ignored its fulminations. We confess that we did not realise the risks of the passive resistance movement in a country like

India. Both the people and their rulers made many mistakes during that period of excitement. And, as Lord Carmichael said very wisely, in Midnapore, people use words and even do things in times of unusual excitement and irritation, which they are, or ought to be, only too glad to forget and mutually forgive, when the excitement is over. This is not the time either for the Government to receive or remember their complaints against popular leaders, nor for these latter, or their friends and following, to fondly cherish the memories of ancient grievances. I am confident that so self-less a public man and patriot like Mr. Tilak does not cherish any sense of his old grievances. He had suffered before for what the Government considered, and a British Judge punished as sedition. But one never heard, I think, from his lips any reference to those sufferings. He took them, clearly, without any ill-will or persistent sense of wrong, as only a part of the day's work. And the man who could rise above these petty and petulant reflections and recollections in his younger days, is not at all likely to harbour or even pay any heed to them now. Mr. Tilak, unless I have entirely misjudged the man, will never allow the memories of the last years, or of the circumstances that brought about his enforced rest, to interfere with the duties that lie before him. If anything caused him pain, it was not so much his personal sufferings or privations,—separation from friends and family—as the break-up of his public activities. And is it too much to hope, and indeed, ask of the authorities that they too will let the dead past bury its dead, and, forgetting the memories of the exciting years that followed the Partition of Bengal, assume a new attitude towards men like Mr. Bal Gangadhar Tilak, whose help and co-operation, it would hardly be politic to refuse at this juncture. Those who have any grasp of the present Indian situation and are able to presage its future, in the light of the unerring trends of the actual evolution of British Imperial politics on the one side, and of general world politics, on the other, cannot, I feel confident, do so.

THE PRESENT DUTY

I have little doubt that Mr. Tilak will

not take long to completely seize the present situation in the country, and the moment he does so, he will not hesitate to recognise and declare the supreme need of amending the Nationlist policy and programme, such as he had known these six years ago—a policy and programme that he had himself done so much to formulate with such unrivalled insight and determination. Mr. Tilak never was a revolutionary. His temperament, his superior native intelligence, his very liberal education, his grasp of the actualities of the political situation in his country, all these are absolutely inconsistent with the very idea of any sort of real revolutionary patriotism. Sir Valentine Chirol, evidently drawing his inspiration from some narrow-visioned Bombay bureaucrats, has completely failed to seize the inner character of this great Brahmin politician. Mr. Tilak is too sane a man to ever dream of reviving for his caste or clan the old power and position of the Peshwas. He knows it, if any Indian does, that unless every historic movement of our time, whether inside or out of India, misses its end, and is turned, by some sudden cataclasm from its own natural and rational course, there is, absolutely, not the ghost of a chance for any particular class or province in India, to lord it over the others. If India ever comes to her own in the future it must be as a whole; and that whole must be, above all else, a federated whole. Every intelligent and educated Indian knows it. Neither Hindus nor Mahomedans, neither Mahrattas nor Sikhs nor even the valour of the Rajputs, could win for their particular community or caste or clan, absolute overlordship in the India of the future. The provinces have had their day,—and the clans and castes too;—the future has been committed to the Indian nation—the complete and composite Indian peoples—composed of Hindus, Moslems, Mahrattas, Sikhs, Tamils, Telugus, Purbiyas and Bengalees. Neither Akbar nor Aurangazeb, neither Shivaji nor Ranjit Singh,—nor, indeed, any one much greater than these, will any more be able to win for themselves the hegemony of the Indian Continent. To think that in these days, when even the Moslem world is alive with the desire for democratic and constitutional ideals of Government, any educated Indian would even dream of any sectional predominance in the coming evolution of Indian history and politics, betrays a strange lack of insight into human nature. Youthful, inexperienced, and imaginative youths, unaffected by any perceptions of the stern and solid actualities of life, might dream such foolish dreams; but the thing is absolutely unthinkable in regard to a man of superior education and intelligence and farsight with which Mr. Tilak is universally credited by both friends and foes. And his native intelligence, his high education, and his firm grasp of the solid realities of life and history, are all against the assumption that he has any real revolutionary aims. Of course, it cannot be denied that, like many others, especially among the thought leaders of the Nationalist movement in India, he too did want to put in some element of self-confidence and even, self-assertiveness, in his countrymen; and in so far as they did it, their words were misread and their real intentions misunderstood by some people, who simply caught their patriotic enthusiasm, without being able to grasp the fundamental psychology or philosophy of national life that really prompted these: and thus turned from steady, sober, but devoted and lawful workers, into violent and hysteric revolutionaries. But this has been almost the universal misfortune of men who have seen far ahead of them, and have tried according to their light, to control the future by seeking to shape the course of the present. What Mr. Tilak saw was the danger with which the inertia and listlessness, the tamasa quality, of the Indian peoples threatened the future peace and progress of his own country. It was a menace, indeed, even to the peace and progress of the Government itself. For it is the universal experience of history that inertia and sexlessness, though they may temporarily smooth the path of autocratic or bureaucratic administrations, ultimately become the parents of violent revolutions. To cure this inertia, and sexlessness of the Indian populations, to lead them to take some active interest in the larger affairs of their state, to train them to habits of independent thinking and self-reliant civic activities, and, through these, to inspire them with a sense of their strength and a vision of their destiny, —these are about the most effective prophylactics against all sorts of revolutionary patriotic outbursts. All these help to humanise historic movements, bring them within the realm of man's rational efforts and activities; while long continued inertia and sexlessness help only to brutalise historic and political reactions. Mr. Tilak must have seen this. Every statesman sees it. Every student of history, who has read his history to any purpose, and has been able to reconstruct ancient evolutions in his own rational life, just as the student of geology reconstructs the pre-historic history of the earth's formation,—every such student of history knows this. And, therefore, in seeking to remove this sexless inertia of his people by an inspiring propaganda of self-reliance and self-help in all civic and political agitations, as against the older propaganda of the Indian National Congress, which had wanted everything or almost everything to be done by the Executive Government in the country, Mr.

Tilak and the other Nationalist leaders followed the only policy that could ensure peaceful progress towards the modern democratic ideal of the state-life and state organisation. If the authorities in Bombay had only realised this, there would have been much saving of trouble and time on both sides.

But, as I said, we must all let by-gones be by-gones. The time has come when Nationalists on the one side, and the Government on the other, should recognise that their interests are not, really, in conflict with one another. The Nationalists must clearly realise it that the only chance of the realisation of their highest ideal of national autonomy, lies, humanly speaking, not in any violent rupture with Great Britain, but in the perpetuation of the British connection. Imperialists must realise it that the self-fulfilment of what they call the British Empire, if not, indeed, its very life and integrity, depends upon the admission of India, by and bye, into an equal co-partnership with the other parts of this Empire. Not what is loosely called colonial self-government, but what is really an Imperial Federation composed of Great Britain herself, and Ireland, and Egypt, and India, and the over-seas Dominions, each autonomous within itself, and absolutely free to manage its own particular affairs, but all combined for purposes of mutual protection and progress, and above all, in the pursuit of those larger humanitarian ends wherein every national life and history must fulfil itself,—this must be accepted as the common ideal-end of both Indian and Imperial evolution. Upon this broad and rational ideal, nationalist and imperialist interests must be completely and permanently reconciled. Both the Government and the people of India must realise it that their future lies not in mutual conflict, but only in reconciliation. I have not the least little doubt in my mind, that Mr. Tilak fully understands this. I am absolutely confident that he is ready and willing to work along this line. An astute politician, a stout thinker, a far-seeing statesman, a selfless patriot, a man who has all his life proved his complete detachment from the fleeting pleasures and pains of life, and has taken all his troubles, smilingly, as in the day's work,—Mr. Tilak cannot possibly refuse to co-operate with the Government, for the furtherance of national autonomy in India and for paving the way to the final organisation of a real Federation in the Empire. The question is : will the authorities in Bombay accept his co-operation ? It will be a great blunder to refuse it. Such a refusal, in any case, any desire to treat him a political suspect, and prevent him free access to the people, will be a very serious loss to the progress of that true, honest, rational and humanitarian nationalism not only on the Bombay side, but, I am afraid, all over India ; for Mr. Tilak is held in very high regard in every Indian province, wherein history must seek and find the greatest safety and the most assured peace for both India and the Empire. Lord Hardinge understands this thoroughly ; and it is to be hoped that His Excellency will see to it that the Provincial Administration allows by-gones to be by-gones, and treats this great leader of his people as a friend, though he has sometimes, to his own cost, played the candid friend to it.

BABU SURENDRA NATH BANERJEE

Whether one agrees with Surendra Nath's public policy or admires his personal character or not, there is one thing which everybody who has any acquaintance with the history of the public life of this country of the last thirty years must admit, namely, that of all Indian public men, he is the only person who may justly claim an all-India leadership. Some of his contemporaries may have a culture much wider than his, others may claim sounder judgment, greater farsight or much superior strength of character than what even the most ardent of Surendra Nath's admirers would venture to prefer for him; some have high professional standing and great wealth at the back of their influence in the political life of their country, others, though without these adventitious advantages, have a reputation for self-less devotion to the country's cause which Surendra Nath may not have acquired in so large a measure: but all these facts notwithstanding, he is, by far and above, the one man in all India, whom if the occasion came, a plebiscite of his English-educated countrymen would with an overwhelming majority acclaim as their trusted leader. Some are leaders of public opinion in their own province, others of their own class or community, a few have even a wider constituency among that large and accommodating body of people who in every Indian Province are always ready to accept the profitable lead of any one who may have won for his public life the recognition of the Government and the official classes; but while the position of all these men in the public life of their country is provincial and sectional, that of Surendra Nath alone is unquestionably, national. And it is only fitting that this should be so; because no other man in his generation or even before him has contributed more to the birth and growth of our present national ideas and aspirations than what Surendra Nath has done.

And the main secret of this unique position that Surendra Nath had undoubtedly secured in the present public life of his country, is to be found, I think, in the peculiar genius and character of the Bengalee people on the one side, and in the special developments of the intellectual and social history of Bengal on the other. Of all the peoples of India, the Bengalee has always been noted for his keen intellectualism and exuberant emotionalism. The mighty military genius of the Punjabee, the incisive practical sense of the Mahratta, the strong metaphysical bent of the Madrasee, and the keen logical acumen of the Bengalee combined with the most fervid emotionalism, stand side by side with one another in the composite character and culture of the Indian people. It has been so in the past ; it is so even to-day. We see it in the different shapes that the same modern spirit, the result of our contact and conflict with the West, has taken in the different Indian provinces. We have, thus, a spirit of active militancy in the propaganda of the Arya Samaj in which the Punjabee element is overwhelmingly preponderant, which is entirely absent from the allied movements of religious and social reform in the other Indian Provinces. Similarly, we have in these same movements in the Mahratta country, neither the spirit of active militancy of the Punjab Arya Samaj nor the frank enthusiasm for the new ideas and ideals that have been characteristic of the Brahmo Samaj in Bengal, but rather a quiet recognition of the inevitable and an attempt to keep as much as possible, the old forms and institutions of the national life, without any fuss, while submitting to the inevitable charges. And this spirit of quiet accommodation and peaceful compromise is born of the strong practical sense of the shrewd Mahratta Brahman. In Madras these movements have so far failed to make any perceptible progress, because, I think, of the simple fact that their representatives and missionaries have so far emphasized only their purely logical and ethical aspects without making any serious attempt to discover and present any broad philosophy of life that may stand behind them. For the Madrasee mind will not accept, nor can be much enthusiastic over anything that does not appeal to its hereditary love for abstruse metaphysical speculations. This is why theosophy, with its metaphysical subtleties on the one side and the supernaturalism and mysticism that go with these everywhere, on the other, has had so far the largest and most enthusiastic following on the Madras side. In Bengal, the movements of the modern thought owing to the peculiar genius of the Bengalee people, have been marked by an uncompromising rationalism on the one hand, and the superb idealism that goes with exuberant emotionalism on the other. In both his religious and his social reform movements, the modern Bengalee has applied with relentless logic the root canons of what is known as modern rationalism in Europe. But he has done so, not in the spirit of modern materialist, whose intellectual standards are almost exclusively sensuous, and whose ethical values always utilitarian, but in that of the idealist who sees beyond the senses, and yearns always for the unattainable.

Logic and law, grammar and rhetoric, ecstatic outbursts more than contemplative quietude in religious life, and impulsive daring rather than calculated courage in affairs: these are the special characteristics of the Bengalee people. It is these that have worked for them the position in which they hold in the present day life and thought of India.

And Surendra Nath is very largely indebted to these characteristics of his race for the unique position that he has made for himself in the public life of his country. He entered that life, while yet a young man, with neither wealth nor rank, nor, as his detractors would perhaps say, with even a good name. A dismissed member of the Indian Civil Service, he has no credit with the Government and the Anglo-Indian community. The Indian press was with the solitary exception of "*The Hindoo Patriot*," without power, and the Indian people without any voice in public affairs. And even the influence of the *Hindoo Patriot* notwithstanding, the exceptional abilities of its Editor, Babu Kristo Das Pal, was due very largely, if not entirely, to its official associations. "*The Amrita Bazar Patrika*" was no doubt coming into prominence by its courageous criticism of official acts and policy, but "*The Patriot*" was the only Indian newspaper that could help make public reputations for our men; and Surendra Nath, when he first commenced to educate public opinion in his country, received precious little help from that quarter. When, thus, upon his return from England after his unsuccessful appeal against the order of his dismissal from the Civil Service, Surendra Nath found himself almost stranded in Calcutta without a decent competence behind and any reasonable expectations before him, and was taken up by Pandit Ishwar Chandra Vidyasagar and provided with a chair in the Metropolitan College at a salary of Rs. 250 a month, no one could predict for him anything like the high position that, in a few short years, he carved for himself in the life and love of his English educated countrymen.

Surendra Nath's unique position in the political leadership of his people, is almost entirely due to his unrivalled powers of eloquence. Judged by some standards, his style of oratory would not, I am afraid, be considered of the highest type. It is very different, for instance, from the style of Edmund Burke, whose words carried his audience with him, not merely by their flow and cadence, but far more, perhaps, by the strength of the facts and arguments that were invariably woven into them. The secret of the great charm that Surendra Nath's oratory exercises over his hearers lies, however, first in his personal magnetism, which is a universal endowment of all powerful leaders of men, and next, in his large wealth of words and imageries whose volume and cadence carry immense audiences before them, like a mighty torrent in high-flood.

In fact, it is not Surendra Nath's style only. It is the common style of what is called the Bengal school of oratory. And this peculiar style has been so wonderfully developed in Bengal for the simple reason that it is best suited to the highly emotional temperament of this people, and for this very reason, it is most effective everywhere in religious preachings. Kesub Chunder Sen regarded by even many cultured Englishmen who heard him speak, as the greatest English orator of his day, was the highest representative of this school. And, as a religious teacher, it suited his vocation most wonderfully. This so-called Bengal School of oratory is, however, ill-suited to the requirements of the political platform; and if, in spite of this fact, Surendra Nath's oratory has been able to achieve so much in our political life, it is partly due to the peculiar temperament of our people, and partly to the special work that Surendra Nath had been called upon to do.

Surendra Nath's style would not suit a sober and responsible deliberative assembly anywhere in modern civilisation. Nor have we had any such institution in our midst when Surendra Nath first entered politics. The work that lay before him was, in fact, not of the statesman or administrator, but of the trumpeteer. And a more powerful trumpet for the call of our new-born patriotism is almost impossible to think of. What was wanted then was not so much the power to think as the capacity to feel. The work before Surendra Nath was, thus, more akin to the religious than to the political. And it is therefore, that his style of oratory became so effective at the time. Neither cold philosophy, nor farseeing statesmanship, nor calculating political schemes could have brought back their normal sensitiveness to a palsied people, or woke up a comatose community. What the situation demanded was the inspiration of an enthralling ideal and the live currents of a lofty and divine enthusiasm. Surendra Nath found these for us; and may well lay claim, therefore, to the distinction of the regenerator of his people.

But Surendra Nath could never have done the work that history will place to his credit if the ground had not been prepared by the succession of great men who preceded him. Chief among the makers of modern Bengal, and to some extent even of Modern India—is Raja Ram Mohun Roy. Ram Mohun is popularly regarded as a great religious and social reformer only. But although owing to the peculiar condition of his times, the public activities of the Raja were more manifest in theological and religious controversies, than in anything else, his real message to his country and, indeed, to the modern world had reference to the entire field of man's social life. In fact, in these theological controversies, he stands far below the plane which he actually occupied, and whence he viewed the world-problem of our time with a breadth of outlook and a depth of insight, rare except among the very greatest of men. He combined in him the fervour of the prophet with the vision of the seer, and the practical sense of the man of affairs with the capacity for grasping the rational grounds of every act or institution, the heritage of the philosopher, the sagacity of the politician with the idealism of the poet. And he was able, therefore, to vitualise the great and complex Indian problem almost in all its phases and departments, and thus to indicate the lines along which it should be approached for satisfactory solution. Others followed him in this work of reform and reconstruction. Harish Chander Mookerjee and Kristo Dass Pal, Debendra Nath Tagore and Keshub Chunder Sen, Ishwar Chandra Vidya-Sagar and Akshoy Kumar Dutt, Hem Chandra Banerjee and Bunkim Chunder Chatterjee, all worked in different departments of the corporate life of their people, and prepared by their labours, the field to which Surendra Nath was called.

In no other province of India have we had, I think, such a long roll of illustrious public men during the latter half of the last century as we had in Bengal. And a new spirit of freedom, more or less strong, characterised the ideals and activities of all of them. Harish Chandra Mookerjee and Kristo Dass Pal, and after them, Sisir Kumar Ghose,—the first two through the "Hindoo Patriot" and the the third through the "Amrita Bazar Patrika"—struck this note of freedom in journalism and politics. The "Hindoo Patriot" had always been very moderate in its tone and cautious in its pronouncements as befitted the recognised organ of the land-owning classes of the Province, whose private interests and public associations both equally demanded it. But the "Patrika" was not hampered by these considerations, and it commenced to give voice to the growing sense of irritation of the English-educated community of the Province caused by their conflicts with the Anglo-Indian Bureaucracy, with an amount of freedom and vigour hitherto unknown in Indian public life. The "Patrika" came to special prominence under the Lieutenant-Governorship of Sir George Campbell (1870-73), whose attempt to restrict higher education with the avowed object of diverting the public funds, thus, set free to the diffusion of primary education, aroused a good deal of opposition from the educated classes. And in their criticism of Sir George Campbell's acts and policy, Babu Sisir Kumar Ghose and his brothers—for the "Patrika" has always been a journalistic joint-family —adopted a tone of biting satire and undisguised abuse, which first shook people's nerves somewhat violently, and then gradually, put a new courage and self-consciousness into them. Debendra Nath Tagore and Keshub Chunder Sen struck a new note of personal freedom in our religious and social life, which even the superior, but essentially synthetic, genius of Raja Ram Mohun Roy had not sought to do; and the spirit of revolt and iconoclasm which these two reformers called into being in the community, soon permeated all the departments of our life and thought. No authority was too high or holy to be touched and tested by human reason: no institution, whether religious or social, too sacred to be allowed to stand out of the melting pot of change and progress, reform and reconstruction. Scriptures and codes, sacraments and ceremonials, customs and institutions, priests and gurus, every one and everything that claimed the holy sanctions of the past, was called upon to present themselves before the Bar of Modern Reason, and either to stand its test or abdicate their authority. This spirit of revolt naturally possessed the soul of our new literature also, and found inspired expression, in prose and verse, through a brilliant group of men, headed by Bunkim Chunder Chatterjee. The "*Bangadharsana*" edited by Bunkim Chunder occupied in the history of the new illumination in Bengal, a position somewhat similar to what the Encyclopædia held in the history of the French illumination of the eighteenth century. It called into being a new school of literary and historical criticism, which though somewhat more conservative than the theological schools of Debendra Nath and Keshub Chunder, was not less rational, and which, because it was somewhat more sober, was not, for that reason, in any way less incisive or vigorous. While the Brahma Samaj Schools applied with relentless vigour the imported canons of the European illuminations of the eighteenth century (modified somewhat partly by their theistic creed and ethical emphasis, and partly by the unconscious influence of the spiritual inheritances of their members) to the demolition of the popular faiths and current customs of the land; the "*Bangadharsana*" applied its own canons to the examination of the claims to superiority of modern European over the old Hindu ideals, and specially, of the presentations of Indian History and the interpretations of Indian culture and civilisation by European students and scholars. And all these various forces intellectual and moral, religious and social, and political, educational and literary, acting and reacting upon one another, gave birth to a new patriotism in the country, which burst forth in song and verse and took complete possession of the educated youths of the nation.

This was the general situation in the country when Surendra Nath entered his public life. The new patriotism had not as yet found a powerful spokesman and leader. It was the beginning almost of what may be called the period of intellection of our new national life. And at this stage of national evolution poetry and drama and even far more than these, public oratory, play a very vital part in helping the development of the new life. Surendra Nath with his unrivalled powers of eloquence came to us, thus, at the very time when our infant patriotism stood in most urgent need of a man like him. And his success was consequently assured from the very beginning of his public career.

Surendra Nath's earliest work was to impart a note of realism to the patriotic inspirations and ideals of his countrymen by relating these to the achievements and actualities of their past and present history. Before Surendra Nath came to the political leadership of his educated countrymen, their patriotism was more or less of a mere airy fairy sentiment, which by its very exuberance tended to undermine its vitality and weaken its capacity to inspire practical activities. Surendra

Nath saved our new patriotism from the inevitable fate of all voluptuous sentimentalism, by imparting to it the inspiration of the actual struggles and achievements of the past on the one hand and calling it to the practical work of the present on the other. His historical addresses, the materials for which he drew partly from Indian and partly from European histories, did the first, and the Students Association, which he started in co-operation with his friend Babu Ananda Mohun Bose, and the Indian Association subsequently organised with the latter as its Secretary did the second part of this much-needed work.

There were political organisations in Bengal even before Surendra Nath's time. But they were more or less class-and-sectional bodies. And the general public, and especially the educated middle classes, were yearning for some adequate and effective organ and organisation of their own to represent the aspirations and interests of the people. And they found it under Surendra Nath's leadership, in the Indian Association. It was no doubt a Bengalee organisation, so far as its actual founders and workers were concerned but as in its name so also in its outlook, the Indian Association was particularly in its early years, unmistakably national. Neither the British Indian Association of Calcutta which is a much older organisation than the Indian Association, nor the Sarbajanik Sabha of Poona, nor even the Bombay Presidency Association which came into existence later, nor the Mahajana Sabha of Madras: none of these had an all-India outlook. They never sought to cover by a network of branch and affiliated institutions, the whole continent, and thereby become a powerful organ of the political life of India as a whole. This conception of the political unity of India has been an original and persistent element of the patriotic ideals and activities of Bengal. It is due to many things—the essentially idealistic temperament of the Bengalee people, the influence of the cosmopolitan sympathies of the Brahmo Samaj, the broader outlook of modern Bengalee literature etc.,—but not the least among these have been the political ideals and aspirations of the teachings of Surendra

Nath. Either from lack of local materials or from the inspiration of a broader ideal, for whatever reasons it may be, Surendra Nath from the very first tried to relate our patriotic sentiments to the past history and achievements of the other provinces of India. And as a result these provincialities worked themselves into our ideals of the future as organic parts of a larger whole, which would incorporate into itself the Punjab and the Mahrashtra, Madras and Rajputana as much as Guzerat and Bengal. The comparatively feebler emphasis of the institution of caste among us, also helped to maintain greater social solidarity, and by keeping us largely free from the conflicts and competitions of inter-caste life and relations gave us a much fuller ideal of political and national unity than what the other Indian provinces had. And all these causes worked together to lend a supremely national meaning and significance to the teachings and activities of Surendra Nath, such as could not, at least in his early days, be claimed for those of any other Indian politician or public man.

In fact, there is every reason to think that if the Indian National Congress had not been started under much greater influential auspices than what Surendra Nath or his friends had then secured for their organisation, and if this new institution, with all its glamour of wealth and rank, and its character as an All-India organisation, had not captivated the imagination of the educated classes, and diverted the course of our political evolution from the less ostentatious but decidedly more vital channels along which it was being quietly directed by the Indian Association—our political activities and organisations would have been, I think, much stronger and of a far more constitutional character than they are to-day. Whatever else the Indian National Congress may or may not have done, of one thing there can possibly be no question whatever, namely, that it has practically killed the natural political life and activities of the people by draining away all the vitality from the local bodies that were being formed under the guidance of the Indian Association, at least all over Bengal and Northern India; and not even the later attempt of the Congress-leaders to build up provincial and district bodies, has so far been or will ever, I am afraid, be able to make up this loss. That which under the healthier influence of the Indian Association, was slowly growing from within the people, the Congress, following the lead of the usual official methods prevalent in this country, has been trying to impose from without.

Indeed, it should not be forgotten that the Indian Association had already started an all-India organisation itself, and a National Conference, to which delegates had been invited by Surendra Nath, from the different districts of Northern India, was actually sitting in Calcutta, when the first Indian National Congress was being almost surreptitiously organised in Bombay. In fact, the Congress was not a people's body from the very start. It was hatched in secret by a few men of great wealth and high professional standing headed by an ex-official of the Government of India. It had thus an aristocratic air about it from the very beginning. And it should be publicly placed on record, before those who know it pass away, that some at least of the most prominent members of the first National Congress which sat in Bombay, deliberately and of set purpose, kept Surendra Nath out of it. It was only when the Congress was proposed to be held next year in Calcutta, and when Mr. Hume saw the utter impossibility of having a successful session in Bengal if Surendra Nath was not taken into the new movement, then he was invited to join it. But though the Congress leaders dared not keep him out, and was subsequently ever ready to exploit Surendra Nath's powers and influence in aid of their work, it is needless to conceive the fact that he never came to the actual leadership of this body, but on the contrary, with the spirit of accommodation, characteristic of the man, he has all along submitted to be led and exploited by his rivals, many of whom never cared even to conceal their want of regard for his personality or their want of appreciation of his worth.

Of course, Surendra Nath like other people, has his limitations. He is not a very cunning politician ; had he been one he would have played his cards better than he has done, and attained to much higher distinctions, as distinctions go in this country, in our present public life. By no means an unaccommodating person, Surendra Nath has never learnt the secret of converting a private surrender to a public victory. He is not a far-seeing statesman either—he does not see all the possibilities of a situation long before they become manifest. He is not even an idealist, who can be oblivious of all practical consequences in his quest for the ideal. He is not a hero who can bravely face the direst personal losses at the call of duty. He is not even a Nationalist in the true sense of the term, for he never learnt anything of his country, its ancient literature and special culture, neither as a youth when he went to school among Anglo-Indians and Eurasians, to the Doveton College, nor in later life, and thus, both by training and heredity, he has been like so many of his contemporaries far too much denationalised to make a true and ideal patriot. But it cannot be however denied that with all his limitations and weaknesses, Surendra Nath has been the one man in our time in this country, who has brought a new life into our politics and who has contributed more than any one else among his contemporaries to make India what it is to-day. He has not given us many ideas, nor much thoughtful leading. But he has given that inspiration without which all else, however valuable in themselves, would be of no earthly use to us or anybody else.

The one fact that stands out therefore, above all things else in the life and work of Surendra Nath Banerjee, is that he occupies a front place among that glorious band, headed by Raja Ram Mohun Roy, whom History will proclaim, to the future generations of this and other lands as the REGENERATORS OF MODERN INDIA.

SRIJUT ASVINI KUMAR DATTA

I

Of the hundreds of letters that I received on my release from prison this time last year, the earliest, and to me, the most valuable, was from this great leader of my people, who is now shut up, without any accusation or trial in the central gaol.

While the rest of my correspondents spoke of *me*, referred to what they called my sufferings and my sacrifices, Asvini Kumar alone spoke not of me but of my Guru and my God.

" Remember, beloved brother," wrote he, " specially at this moment when the whole country is giving you such a hearty ovation, that you are a mere instrument in the hands of Him who is the Master of your life and your destiny. Remember Him always, and neither honour nor dishonour will make any difference to you."

Asvini Kumar is presented by the irritated officialdom in India and the ignorant Jingo press in England as a mischievous political agitator. But his people know him to be a lover of God and man of God. The species, political agitators, is unknown in India. Politics is not as yet a profession in our country, except, perhaps among the very few who are members of the Legislative Councils, and whose official associations sometimes help them to make an addition to their income by writing petitions and memorials on behalf of the princes and the nobility to the Government. But the member of Council is a respectable man and not a pestilential demagogue. Asvini Kumar, had he been so minded, might have been one of these, but instead of earning any money through his public activity, he has all his life spent his own substance in serving his country.

Our civilisation is such that whoever works for the public must either bear all the expenses of his public services himself, or, if he is too poor to do so, he must depend upon what comes to him unasked and unsought as the means of his subsistence. Work that is paid for is mercenary, and has no virtue in it. Every labourer may be worth his hire, but he who stipulates for his hire or refuses to accept whatever comes of itself, works for himself and not for God. Christian God is proud of her own George Muller, but in heathen India, whoever consecrates himself to the service of his fellow-men, which is really the service of God, has of necessity to be a George Muller. Political agitators, therefore, in the European sense of the term, have absolutely no place in the scheme of our national activities. And Asvini Kumar is, in no sense of the term, a political agitator.

Born of rich parents, Asvini Kumar was laid under no necessity to work for a living. Not blessed with any children he had not to provide for the future of even a large family. Without any son, he adopted, one might say, the entire school-going population of his district as his own, and devoted all his substance to their education. He started a school in Barisal, which gradually developed into a college, and stands now as one of the high, most efficient and popular private educational institutions affiliated to the Calcutta University. Asvini Kumar has never sought to convert his school or college as a source of private income, has never conducted them along trade lines. For years together he bore all the deficits himself, living a plain life, and devoting practically all his income to the equipment and upkeep of his educational institution.

A distinguished graduate of the Calcutta University, he has personally supervised and directed the work of his school and college, devoting the best part of his time to his boys. Endowed with a magnetic personality he has been a guide, philosopher and friend to the thousands of young men who have, during the last twenty-five years, passed through his school and college. His students are spread all over Eastern Bengal to-day, occupying important positions in the various walks of life and it is these men who really constitute the very backbone of the Nationalist Movement in that Province.

Modern education in India is oftentimes condemned as a godless education. It is essentially secular; and if secular education be a proper synonym for godless education, the Indian system may be called so. In truth, however its godlessness is due more to godless men who are placed so often in charge of it, and to the character of the education itself. Theology may be taught by means of selected text-books; but real godliness proceeds only from soul to soul. A godly teacher develops the most fervent piety even through a secular system of education, while a godless will desecrate the highest theological text-books by his irreverent life and conversation. Asvini Kumar's personality imparted a truly religious tone to most of his pupils, such as even few denominational schools or professedly theological seminaries are able to do.

Like all spiritual-minded young men of a generation, Asvini Kumar also was in his youth a follower of the Brahmo Samaj, at that time under the leadership of Keshub Chunder Sen. He did both join the Brahmo communion, which would involve separation from his family and social excommunication. Brahmo Samaj stands for rational religion on the one side, and social reform on the other; and in both, it is more alike to European thought and ideal than to the Indian culture and traditions. Asvini Kumar, in his mature years, found it difficult to accept the essentially didactic rationalism of prevailing Brahmo theology as truly rational, and gradually drifted into the great Bhakti Movement of Pundit Bijoy Krishna Goswami. Pundit Bijoy Krishna had himself been in his earlier life a leader of the Brahmo Samaj. As an apostle of that creed, he was for many years intimately associated with Keshub Chunder Sen. But the creed of the Brahmo Samaj was too narrow to the rich, the varied, and the deep spiritual experiences of this great spiritual teacher, and he gradually found himself the centre of a new and powerful religious movement in Bengal, which revived the fervent spirituality of the old Vaishnavic movements, giving a new meaning and interpretation in our age, to ancient thought and experience. Asvini Kumar was drawn to this great teacher, and deeper inspirations of his life henceforth flowed from this source.

To the outside public of Bengal, Asvini Kumar is known as a great educationist, but to those who have come into close personal contact with him, he is known, revered, and loved as a student of religion and an earnest and devout seeker after

God. In Bengali literature he is known as the author of a rich and learned compendium on Bhakti Yoga or the Way of Love. I call it a compendium because the author has copiously drawn from the ancient literature of Bhakti in India; but it is more than a compendium. It is not a mere anthology, but a luminous exposition, largely in the light of personal spiritual experiences of the author himself, of the ancient ideal of Bhakti and the various methods by which it is to be cultivated and attained. It is in this book, apart from his personal life and conversation that we see the inner soul of Asvini Kumar.

Bhakti, or love of God, assumes many forms in India, but the highest of these is what has been summed up in the Bhagavat Gita specially in the twelfth chapter of that immortal book. The ideal lover of God, the devotee—most approved of the God=Lord—is he "who harbours no ill-feeling towards any creature, man or beast; who is friendly towards all and has pity for all; who is without any conceit of self and any selfish attachment; who is indifferent equally to pain and pleasure; who is uniformly forgiving and forbearing; who is content with whatever he gets; who is the master of his senses, strong in his faith, living in a perpetual consciousness of the presence of the Divine; and, who has consecrated his mind and understanding to the Lord; by whom no creature is troubled and whom the creatures cause no trouble; who is free from exultation and depression, fear and anxiety." In another place it is laid down that the ideal devotee is he who realises the presence of the Lord in his own self as well as in every other creature, and whose activities are all consecrated to the service of the Lord.

This has been the ideal of the life of Asvini Kumar for many years past. His personal devotions, his family relations, his social and even his political activities have been guided by this lofty ideal. The inspiration of this consecrated life and labours has always flowed from this divine ideal.

For some years past, Asvini Kumar has been engaged in writing a supplementary volume to his Bhakti Yoga, under the name of Karma Yoga, or The

Way of Works. Bhakti is essentially a concern of the emotional life, while Karma is that of the volitional life. The conception of Karma has had a wonderful evolution in Hindu thought and disciplines. Originally, it meant sacrificial works. The Bhakti schools very largely discarded the ancient sacrifices, and interpreted Karma as the worship of the Lord through his symbols. Higher Vaishnavic thought added to these ceremonial duties, the service of man. Finally, in the latest synthesis of Raja Ram Mohan Roy, Karma has been interpreted as every thing that furthers the highest good of the people. Asvini Kumar has so sought to combine the highest ideal of public duty as conceived by European thought, with the profound spirituality and the lofty ideals of Bhakti of his people. To him, the whole world is a manifestation of the Lord. King and subject, master and servant, the oppressor and the oppressed, he who gives and he who receives, all these various phases of public life and activity, as well as all the varieties of private life and relations, whether they be of the friend and friend, or teacher and pupil, or parent and child, or husband and wife—are all manifestations of Divine Leela or the Sport of the Lord. Neither politics nor economics has, therefore, been a mere secular concern with Asvini Kumar.

A man guided by such ideals and principles often times lays open to popular misunderstanding and misconception. Asvini Kumar has also been repeatedly misunderstood even by his closest friends and most ardent admirers. Ordinarily public men may be divided into two classes, the impulsive and the calculative. Superficially judged, Asvini Kumar would seem to have a large doze of both in the composition of his mind and character. Sometimes he appears to be highly impulsive, and other times almost repulsively calculating. In his private relations he is almost as gushing as a woman. You cannot approach the man without feeling the excessive warmth of his heart. Yet when it is a question of public duty, he is often times found to hector and hesitate to take a decisive step such as appears to be absolutely imperative to more impulsive men. I have repeatedly experienced both these sides of the character of Asvini Kumar, and have sometimes mis-judged his public acts.

He was so mis-judged by a very large section of his own people in the winter of 1904—5, over the incidents that took place at Barisal on the occasion of Sir Bamfylde Fuller's visit to that town as Lieutenant-Governor of the newly formed province of Eastern Bengal and Assam. Barisal has been the stronghold of the Boycott Movement ever since it was started. And the magnetic personality of Asvini Kumar has been the central force of it. There, Asvini Kumar has for many years past been the idol of the people of Barisal, including the classes and the masses both. His word was law to the people ; and when he declared that no one should buy or sell foreign goods any more, most people accepted it at once as a sacred injunction. It was not the result of any terror that the boycotters had established in the town, but was simply the natural result of the loving regard in which the people held their leader. A European resident of the place wanted a few yards of grey shirting, and sent his servant to the market to buy a piece. But no one would sell any foreign goods. The matter was reported to the Superintendent of Police, and he sent a constable to the market to buy a piece of Manchester shirting for his friend. The constable was no more successful than the servant. Every trader refused to sell any foreign cloth without a permit from Asvini Babu. The matter was reported to the magistrate, who wrote a letter to Asvini Kumar, and asked him for a permit for a piece of Manchester shirting for his European friend. This had happened a few weeks before the new Lieutenant-Governor started upon his tour.

The incident, apparently so insignificant, was naturally regarded as very serious by the authorities. It showed on the one hand the tremendous possibilities of the Boycott Movement in Bengal; on the other hand, it was a sign of the dangerous decline of the prestige and moral authority of the British executive in Barisal. It showed that while the magistrate was the ruler of the district, Asvini Kumar really controlled the sentiments and activities of the people. In constitutional and democratic countries, such idols of the people become by an easy and natural process the rulers of the state; and personal regards strengthen the root of political obligations. Under a despotic administration, where there is natural conflict, whether latent or patent, between the will of the people and the authority of the state, whoever gains any stronghold in the popular mind becomes a distinct menace to the authority and prestige of the Government, unless he identifies himself with that government, and lends it completely and unreservedly the support of his personal influence. At one time Asvini Kumar had done so. He was at one time associated with the district executive in municipal and local administration. But he was no longer their associate. The Partition of Bengal had created a violent breach between the administration and the people of the province. Asvini Kumar took his stand in this conflict against the Government. He was, so to say, the head of the opposition, in his own district, if not in the whole of East Bengal. His hold on his people, the unique regard in which he was held alike by the classes and the masses of his district, the ready obedience that they rendered to his requests, constituted thus a serious menace to the authority and prestige of the bureaucracy. Asvini Kumar's power over his people had to be crushed.

This was the idea with which, it seems, Sir Bamfylde Fuller went to receive his instructions from the retiring Viceroy Lord Curzon who was then at Agra. Sir Bamfylde's position had been made exceedingly unpleasant by the organised refusal of the people of the new province to give him the equal honour which the Governors of Indian provinces had been accustomed to receive. At Dacca the public practically refused to accord him a fitting reception. To add to his irritation, while he was received on his arrival at the town by scarcely four or five hundred people, most of whom were Mahomedans brought together by the personal influence of the Nawab of Dacca, a Nationalist work coming in the next day was received at the station by over five thousand people, and while the Lieutenant Governor's state barge was lying on the river, an anti-partition demonstration was held under his very nose in which from ten to fifteen thousand people were present. This was, as Sir Bamfylde Fuller himself declared, more than what even an angel could bear. When he went to Faridpur, it was reported in the newspapers, that even the railway porters refused to touch his luggage, which had to be carried by police-constables. From Faridpur Sir Bamfylde went to meet Lord Curzon at Agra. What passed there in secret consultation between the retiring Viceroy, who was responsible for the Partition of Bengal, and the Lieutenant-Governor, no one knows. But it was published in the papers that from Agra, Sir Bamfylde ordered for the despatch of a hundred Gurkhas, to Barisal. Sir Bamfylde went from Agra to Barisal, and while the hundred military police were drawn up on the river bank, he invited Asvini Kumar and other local leaders to a conference on board his state barge and there insulted them openly, and threatened them with immediate arrest unless they withdrew a certain circular issued by them to the people, advising them the legality of a peaceful boycott of the British goods.

Had Asvini Kumar refused to withdraw that circular, the history of Sir Bamfylde's first visit to Barisal would have been differently written. The whole town was in the ferment, and the arrest of Asvini Kumar at that time would have resulted in serious riot, which even Sir Bamfylde's hundred Gurkhas would have found it impossible to quell. Asvini Kumar saw the prospects of all this carnage, and decided even to be adjudged a coward rather than, however indirectly, be the cause of a blood riot in his own town. No demagogue ever thinks in this way. Few politicians in the position of Asvini Kumar in any part of the world would have exercised such forbearance and sacrificed their public character for the sake of public peace. A self-assertive man would have defied the Lieutenant-Governor and would have earned cheap martyrdom by going to prison for his refusal to withdraw an absolutely legal circular, though such a refusal might lead to bloodshed among the reckless and excited populace. Asvini saved the situation in Barisal by forbearance.

Sir Bamfylde won an apparent victory, but it was after all a mere physical victory. The moral victory was with Asvini Kumar. For though Asvini Kumar gave in to the bullying of the Lieutenant-Governor there was no demoralisation either in him or in his people. Sir Bamfylde left his Gurkhas behind him in Barisal, and for some weeks they established what was described in the papers of the time a regular reign of terror in the town. Barisal has always been noted for its population, and yet that among such a population a handful of Gurkhas could commit such outrages as were reported in the papers from day to day, showed the moral hold of Asvini Kumar upon his people, and the restraining influence he has always been among them. Asvini Kumar saw through the game of the executive. The object of this Gurkha rule was clearly to exasperate the people and drive them to acts of lawlessness, such as would provide the Government with a decent plea to crush the Swadeshi Movement there with sheer force, and he refused to be played in the hands of his opponents. Though the Gurkhas committed many excesses, the people did not overstep the limits of law in a single instance. Their forbearance indeed had a tremendous moral influence on the Gurkhas themselves, and they had subsequently to be withdrawn from Barisal. Asvini Kumar's anxiety to avoid almost at any cost, any kind of physical conflict with the authorities was seen again when the Provincial Conference met the following year April 1906 (8: Barisal). This gathering was broken up by the order of the magistrate almost on the point of the bayonet. A procession of nearly eight or nine hundred delegates from the different districts of the province, including almost every prominent leader of the country, was also dispersed by the Police who made a free use of their quarter staff and broke more than a head, under the very eyes of the District Superintendent of Police. The processionists were not even summoned to disperse peacefully and voluntarily. Asvini Kumar has simply to raise his little finger and the excited populace of the town would have crushed the small band of police and all the executive officials like dry leaves in the hollow of a man's hand. But he was determined that the movement with which he was connected should never be identified with any form of lawlessness, and his forbearance, misinterpreted by many ardent young men at the time as cowardice, saved the situation in Barisal once more on that day.

But while he refused to have his people driven to any form of lawlessness, either by the insults of the Lieutenant-Governor or the unprovoked assaults of the local executive, he never loosened his hold or allowed his people to loosen their hold of the weapon of peaceful and lawful passive resistance. The more the official became lawless the stronger became the Boycott Movement in Barisal. And in no Bengal district had this prosecution of this economic boycott been so little associated with any sort of violence and illegality as in Barisal. And the secret of it is to be found in the personal character and influence of this great leader of his people.

Asvini Kumar is indeed a born leader of men. He is the only real leader that we have had as yet in Bengal, for he is the one man who may be said to possess a large and powerful following. And the secret of this is his character. Even his rankest enemies—and in modern public life, even the best and sweetest of men cannot altogether avoid making a few enemies—havenever found any reason to insinuate any unworthy motive or act to Asvini Kumar. But purity alone, however much it may command admiration, does not always draw people's hearts. The secret of Asvini Kumar's influence is not merely the purity of his life, but, above all, the genuine sweetness of his disposition. Asvini Kumar knows how to be a boy among boys, a youth among young men, and an aristocrat among aristocrats, and a genuine proletariat among the proletariat. He is a Hindu among Hindus. And he knows also how to feel, how to think, and even talk like a Mahomedan among Mahomedans.

One little incident that occurred a little over a year ago may be mentioned as showing the inner character of the man, and the secret of his wonderful influence over his people. A person belonging to the Namasudra class, which may be said to constitute almost the very backbone of the Hindu peasantry of Barisal and other eastern districts of Bengal, but who are usually considered as very low in the social scale, went one day to see Asvini Kumar. Asvini Kumar was at that time living in a house boat, and touring about the district. As soon as this man went and accosted Asvini Kumar, he returned his salute, and coming down from his chair took his seat alongside of his visitor in the same carpet. When Asvini Kumar asked him concerning the object of his visit, the man said :—" I came to ask a question, but it has already been answered, and I have no need of troubling you any more about it."

Asvini Kumar was surprised at the remarks, and asked his visitor to explain himself. The man said that he had been told by some people that this cry of "Bande Mataram" was a mere humbug, for if the country be our Mother we must then be all brothers, but how then do the higher classes refuse to accept the lower classes as such? This question puzzled him, and he had come to Asvini Kumar for a solution of it. But Asvini Kumar by leaving his seat and receiving a Nama-Sudra peasant as his equal had answered the question practically.

To Asvini Kumar every religion, so far as it proclaims the glory of God and preaches His Love, is true. To him, therefore, it makes but little difference whether God is worshipped in a temple, a mosque or a church. To him every man is the image of his Maker, a symbol of God. The service of man is the service of the Lord. Family affections, social re-actions, economic arrangements, and political ordinances are all means for the realisation of the highest love of God. And this essentially religious spirit is the secret of his wonderful influence over a people with whom religion counts as the highest factor in life. The character of every public movement is best revealed in the character of its leaders. In Asvini Kumar we have a most convincing proof of the profound spirituality of the present Nationalist Movement in Bengal.

SRIJUT ASVINI KUMAR DATTA

II

Babu Asvini Kumar Datta holds a somewhat unique position among his colleagues in the leadership of the present public life of his Province. They are almost all, without a single exception, leaders of the English-educated middle class only. Asvini Kumar is the only person, who has a large and devoted following among the masses. The leadership of the classes is won by large intellectual powers, superior gift of eloquence, and sometimes also by high professional or official standing, or even by large wealth, discriminately used to advance and control public activities. Asvini Kumar lays claim to none of these. A man of considerable intellectual power, he is not a recognised intellectual force among his people. Intellectual leadership comes either through the press or through the platform. Asvini Kumar has written an excellent book on BHAKTI YOGA which shows the deep religious bent of his soul and extensive religious reading, especially in our ancient Bhagavata literature ; but he has not a high and recognised position in Bengalee literature. He is a good and effective speaker, but his eloquence is not of that class which moves an audience by its sheer magnetic force and takes them off their feet and compels them to accept any doctrine or pursue any ideal with all their mind and strength. Like Bal Gangadhar Tilak, Asvini Kumar did take his law degree, and thus fully qualified himself for the legal profession, but never seriously practised law, and so did not win any professional distinction, though it was within easy reach of him. His father was a distinguished member of the Government service in East Bengal, and he too, if he cared for it, might have taken service under the Government, where his intellectual and moral qualifications could have easily won for him great distinction. But he preferred to live and die a private gentleman, upon the fair competence that his father left him. But he did not, for that reason, choose to lead an idle life. His paternal estate was not very large according to present day estimates, but it was sufficiently large to keep him and his people, not only above want but in comparative affluence also. Asvini Kumar has no children, and freed from all parental responsibility, he might well have lived in Calcutta on the income of his estate, and thrown himself, like some other Bengal zemindars, into the virtues and vices of the present day absentee land-lordism. But he preferred, instead, to live in the comparative obscurity and seclusion of his own town, with his own people, in close and intimate touch with his tenantry, devoting his time, his talents, his money to the service of his people and his country. And this is why Asvini Kumar is the only man to-day in Bengal who may be truly said to be a popular leader, and not, in any sense of the term, a mere political, agitator

In our old society, before the break-up of our old village life, title to leadership was always based upon personal relationship between the leader and his following. It was also the title to leadership of the old feudal lords in Europe. It is the character of the true leadership of the military officer, among his soldiery.

And this paternal element makes this kind of leadership a live and sensitive thing. The modern political leader is of quite a different character. Organisations, when they are developed and perfected into a mighty machine tend always to kill this personal element in human relations. Organised public life or political agitation, needs, therefore, but little direct personal relationship between the leader and his following. The nature of the leadership of comparatively simpler and primitive communities was very different. Not high intellectual powers expressed through the national literature, nor "the divine gift of the gag,"—neither superior erudition nor large wealth—none of these were essential qualifications for leadership in our old social life. But unblemished character, unshaken and unshakable honesty, broad sympathies, and devoted social service—homely and unostentatious—these were the highest title to leadership among our primitive people. The relation between the leader and his following was not a platform relation, whose only field was the Committee-Room or the Meeting Hall, but a living, sensitive, personal bond. The real leader of the ryot was not the man who only owned his fields and received the rents; but he who won his heart. More often than not, the zemindar of the village was also the leader of the villagers; but that was because he was, in the first place, a comparatively small land-owner, and secondly, because, he never lived away from his tenantry. The zemindar, who lived in his own estate, among his own tenants, was always a man of simple habits and primitive manners. He shared his wealth, in a thousand ways with his ryots. He was always accessible to them, and his house was always open to them. They came to his feasts, and participated in his festivals. His fish-pond and even his fruit orchard were, in a sense, the common property of his people; they freely came with their rod to catch fish in his pond, and their children had free access to the fruits in his garden. He always addressed the meanest and poorest of his tenants, if they were older than himself—irrespective of all considerations of their caste—as brother or cousin, paternal or maternal uncle, and they too reciprocated the sentiment by accepting this relationship. He was an intimate guest in their marriages and *shradhas* and a kindly, friendly, visitor in their lowly homes, whenever death or misfortune cast its shadows over them. This was the old ideal of leadership in our country. The elders of every village were thus the natural leaders of their people. And Asvini Kumar is the only man among the well-known leaders in Bengal, who can justly lay some claim to this natural leadership in our generation. He has lived all his life among his own people, lived like them in every way identified with their joys and their sorrows, and one might say, with their merits and their demerits as well. He has gone up to them, talked with them in their native patois, sat with them in the shade of their mango, topes or the clean-swept yards of their thatched huts. His going among them has been like that of a personal and trusted friend. They have always opened their hearts to him, as they would never do to any other man, neither zemindar nor tahsildar, neither priest nor padre; and he too gave them freely of his love and sympathy. This is the secret of the unique influence that Asvini Kumar has over the masses in his district. They talk of uncrowned kings. So far as I know, Asvini Kumar is the only public man in India, who has a just title to this distinction.

This is why the Swadeshi movement took such deep roots in Asvini Kumar's district, Barisal. In Barisal Swadeshi became almost a religion among the masses, and people took to it, without question, and yet with such stern determination, simply because Asvini Kumar was its high priest. This is why, again, even during the most exciting periods in 1907, 1908 and 1909 when people got out of hand in Calcutta and Dacca and other places and committed themselves to a course of violence and lawlessness which never had the sanction of leaders of the new movement in Bengal, Barisal was singularly free from these excesses. Neither Calcutta nor Dacca or any other district had real swadeshi leader, whose word was the law to the people, and without whose direct command no man would do anything. Neither Surendra Nath in Calcutta, nor Ananda Chandra Roy, nor

Ananda Chandra Chakravarti at Dacca, nor Ananth Bandhu Guha in Mymensingh, nor any one in Comilla, had the fullest confidence of the people, both young and old, both educated and uneducated, as Asvini Kumar had in Barisal. This is the real cause of all the troubles that we had almost all over Bengal, except Barisal. And yet we all know it that nowhere in West Bengal, or East Bengal has the swadeshi sentiment been stronger, or the swadeshi determination sterner than it has always been in Asvini Kumar's district. The credit of it is due entirely to the personal character of this true and real leader of his people, and the salutary and restraining influence which he has always exercised over them.

Twice did Asvini Kumar save the situation, not merely in Barisal but to some extent in the whole of Bengal, under the exciting and troublous administration of Lord Minto. The first was during Sir Bamfylde Fuller's visit to Barisal, in November 1905, when the Lieutenant Governor of the new Province of Eastern Bengal and Assam invited the leaders of the district to his yacht, abused them like school boys, and threatened to order their immediate arrest, unless they did his bidding and publicly withdrew a certain circular that had been sent out above their signatures, proclaiming that it was not unlawful for anybody to refuse to buy foreign goods, if he wanted to do so. Popular leaders had never before been treated to such open insults by any official of Sir Bamfylde's standing. The thing was unknown in the history of the British administration, at least, in Bengal. And we owed it to Asvini Kumar's marvellous self-restraint and statesmanly far-sight that in consequence of this act of the new Lieutenant-Governor, the town, and indeed, the whole district were not made over to fatal disorder, bordering almost upon an open revolt, that day. Sir Bamfylde Fuller, exasperated by the "boycott" that was declared against him in almost every Eastern District, completely forgot himself. He forgot his position as the King's representative; he forgot his responsibility for the peace and good Government of the people committed to his charge; he forgot his duties as the official host of respectable leaders of the country; and he forgot the fact that evil developments might arise if these leaders openly resented such unseemingly treatment and refused to submit to the angry threats of the Lieutenant-Governor. Sir Bamfylde forgot all this, but Asvini Kumar did not; and this is how the situation was saved that day. Asvini Kumar knew the illegality of the gubernatorial threat. He knew that Sir Bamfylde might order his arrest, but the order would not stand good in law. He knew that he had done nothing to support a lawful conviction against him. And he knew that to drive the Lieutenant-Governor to this act of extreme folly would have been to put him in the wrong before all the world. To a politician of the demagogue type, the temptation to do this would have been simply overwhelming. But Asvini Kumar is not a demagogue. Had Asvini Kumar cared more for his personal reputation than for the peace and happiness of his people, he would have refused to submit to Sir Bamfylde's threats. And the result would have been a frightful riot in Barisal and in the whole of Backerganj district, if not in other places also in Bengal, which would have been found impossible to quell without serious bloodshed. Asvini Kumar saw it all, and he unhesitatingly sacrificed his reputation for courage by agreeing to obey Sir Bamfylde's illegal order in the interest of the peace of his district. And this sacrifice, by no means an easy one for a popular leader, saved the situation in Barisal that day. And he saved the situation not only in Barisal, but in Bengal, similarly, a few months later, when the Provincial Conference was broken up, and a peaceful procession of the delegates forcibly dispersed by the police, in April 1906. All this shows the character and calibre of the man.

In fact Asvini Kumar is not a political agitator of the type with which we are so familiar in Europe. He has not the making of the demagogue in him but rather of the patriarch. A demagogue has the gift of the gab; Asvini Kumar, as I have said, is no orator. A demagogue is reckless of all consequences; Asvini Kumar though he has not been mindful of his personal profit or comforts and has always been free with his purse to promote the public good, is not impervious to considerations of consequences. He thinks long before he acts; and though by nature he is a man of impulse, his impulses are always kept within bounds by his strong common sense and his innate fear of wrong and injustice.

Early in life Asvini Kumar came under the influence of the Brahmo Samaj and it was thought at the time that he would join the Brahmo Communion also. But while the rational and spiritual ideals of the Samaj impressed him strongly, Asvini Kumar lacked courage to openly join the social revolt of the movement, and so at the bidding of his father, he quietly went and married in orthodox Hindu fashion after the rules of his own caste. And so far as I know, Asvini Kumar has done nothing since then which the progressive conscience of his community does not openly tolerate. The fact really is that Asvini Kumar has not in him the stuff of which rebels are made. His enemies say he is too invertebrate to boldly stand up against the existing order, however much he might feel its evil effect. His friends say he is too conscientious to adopt any anti-social course.

And the secret of it is to be found in his religious philosophy and the disciplines which he adopted for the regulation of his inner life. As a young man, like most young men of his generation as the result of his English education, Asvini Kumar also caught the contagion of the European Rationalism of the last century, and thus set up his individual conscience as the ultimate arbiter of both what is true and what is good. The individualistic rationalism of the 18th and the 19th centuries ignored the fact that neither our individual reason nor our individual conscience, works by itself, but is practically dependent for its conclusions upon what may be called the social reason and social conscience. Our intellectual beliefs and our moral intuitions are always derived, however unconsciously it may be, more or less from our racial and communal inheritances and our social institute and institutions. We have the same mind, the same psychological and emotional constitution as other humans, yet we do not hold everything that they believe, as true or reasonable. This is why there are different systems of philosophies in different countries, and wide divergencies of opinion among the most thoughtful and the learned even in the same country. The same is true of our moral institutions also. What is regarded as virtue in one community is condemned as vice in another. There is no uniformity of moral standards in this world, any more than there is of intellectual tests. And it shows that individual reason and individual conscience are not really free-agents but are always influenced by the society to which the individuals belong. Our natural environments also have a lot to do with our moral life. And all these considerations, gradually developing a new science both of thought and society, are forcing a reconsideration of the individualistic rationalism of the last two centuries, and proving the inadequacy of the earlier philosophy of our own Brahmo Samaj also. Asvini Kumar almost instinctively recognised this weakness of the Brahmo Samaj. He saw that the inevitable logic of the position, which the Brahmo Samaj took up, from the time of the Maharshi Debendra Nath Tagore, was philosophical anarchism. Practically the Brahmo Samaj did not work out this logic. It has set up a creed of its own, by which the conclusions of individual reason and individual conscience are practically tested. But in setting up this creed, the Samaj has acted not logically, but arbitrarily. This creed represents the concensus of *opinion* of the generality of members of the Samaj, regarding the Dogmas of religion. The opinion of the majority of the members of the Samaj is the ultimate authority and the highest credential of the validity of the Brahmo dogmas. Ruskin says that ten fools can never make one wise man. But the cruel logic of the individualistic rationalism when organised into a Church, with its dogmas, disciplines, rituals and sacraments, is—that ten fools *must*, because they are ten and not eight, be wiser than nine wise men. Asvini Kumar like many others saw the inherent unreason of this position, and went in search of a more rational basis for authority in religion. He found it in the Hindu doctrine of the *Guru*. And in his allegiance to his *Guru* and the profound spiritual inspiration that he received from him, we must seek for the real key to the complexities, and even the apparent contradictions of his character.

This Hindu doctrine of the *Guru* is practically unknown to the other world cultures. The nearest approach to the inner philosophy of this doctrine is found in the Christian doctrine of Christ, as preached by the Alexandrian Fathers, and as has been latterly developed, under the influence of modern rationalism in some of the Christian philosophers of the Intuitionist School, notably in Mansell and M'cCosh. There is, according to this doctrine a dual manifestation of Christ—one in the consciousness of individual humans, the other in history. The Christ in consciousness and the Christ of history are one and the same. The one is subjective and the other is objective: that is all the difference between them; and they are both one with the Father or the Absolute. They are both manifestations of the Father. This, briefly and in plain language, is the ancient Alexandrian and the modern Intuitionist doctrine of the Christ. The Hindu doctrine of the *Guru* is based upon the same logic of thought, and seeks to offer the same explanation practically of the same problem of the spiritual life. But while the Christ in consciousness in an ever increasing revelation whose manifestation is unbroken and continuous, knows neither completeness nor finality, the historical Christ was revealed once for all, two thousand years ago, in Judea and worked the final atonement of man with God at Calvary. The Hindu doctrine coincides fully with the first half of this Christian doctrine. The Christ-in-Consciousness of Christian experiences is called "chaityaguru" (चैत्य गुरू) the Guru-in-Consciousness by the Hindu. But the objective or the "mohanta-garu" (मोहान्त गुरू) the Guru-in-practical life or the Guru in the flesh of Hindus is not one revelation but a succession of revelations. Even at the same moment of time he is not revealed in one individual but in many individuals to meet the varied requirements of different natures and cultures. The Hindu recognises the absolute need of objective stimuli for the growth and evolution of subjective intuitions. But these intuitions are not identical in all men; consequently, their objective stimuli also cannot be identical. What will stimulate one man's intuitions will not necessarily stimulate another's. So you want, really, as many historical Christs as there are men, and there must be at least one historical incarnation in every age and epoch if not in every country and culture, as otherwise the value of the historic revelation is lost. The Hindu recognised this difficulty. Therefore he believes in many incarnations, and many gurus though at the back of all this multiplicity there is the same Unity of the Absolute. The relation between a man and his *Guru* is an intimate *personal* relation. The true *Guru* reveals that much of himself to his disciple as is suited to the requirements of the inner life of the latter. To be an objective revelation of God, the *Guru* must be a man, and thus stand before the disciple in the flesh. This is absolutely necessary, especially for those, whose sense of identity between the soul and the body has not been cancelled and destroyed by long and laborious, physical, psycho-physical, mental, ethical and spiritual disciplines. In this, the Hindu doctrine of the *Guru* seems to be much fuller and more rational, that is more self-consistent than the Christian doctrine of the Christ, both Catholic and Protestant. And it is here that Asvini Kumar at last found a solution of his religious difficulty and a basis for his spiritual life.

And the secret of Asvini Kumar's character and personality is to be found, I think, in his self-consecration to his *Guru*. This self-consecration is not yet full and complete; but the desire to consecrate himself absolutely to his *Guru* is responsible for all the struggles of his life, and also for the apparent weaknesses and indecisions of his character. By nature a man of sentiment, and therefore necessarily impulsive, his conscientious desire to follow in the steps of his *Guru*, interferes with the unrestrained play and fulfilment of his impulses, and leads to what appears to outsiders as vacillation and weakness. Asvini Kumar's own nature prompts him to adopt a certain course of action. But he asks, it seems, what would my *Guru* do in the circumstance?

And the question leads to hesitancy, doubt, indecision, ultimately, even to a wrong course. And in spite of all his inherited Hindu instincts and his extensive studies of Hindu scriptures, Asvini Kumar appears here, more as a pious Christian than as a true Hindu disciple of the highest order. He forgets that we are not like our *Guru* and cannot, therefore, naturally which means legitimately in the highest sense of the term, follow the course that he would have followed under the same circumstances. The very desire is almost blasphemous. The attempt is sinful, because it is the attempt of the lower to over-ride his own proper law and adopt that of the higher. Judged in the light of Christian legalism, Asvini Kumar's is a very high type of character. He has a keenly sensitive conscience. He is always afraid of doing anything which is not absolutely right. And his objective standard of right is the life and character of his *Guru* even as that of the Christian is the life and character of Christ. But it is not, however, the highest type of Hindu piety or Hindu discipleship. The highest type of Hindu piety and the highest ideal of Hindu discipleship is to consecrate not only our will and our acts, but also our reason and our emotions and our conscience to the *Guru*. In one sense, this is the highest Christian ideal also. The devout Christian—with whom Christ's atonement and sacrifice are not mere outward creeds and dogmas but realities of his own inner spiritual experience—having consecrated himself to his Master, takes no more thought, really, of either sin or virtue but lives in the absolute assurance that all his sins, actual and possible have been washed away in the blood of the Son of God. And there is really little or no difference between him and the true Hindu disciple who views his living *Guru* whom he has seen in the flesh, in the same light as the Christian views his Christ. This Hindu disciple's motto is :—

जानामि धर्म्मं नच मेप्रवृत्ति :
जानाम्यधर्म्मं नच मेनिवृत्ति : ।
त्वया हृषिकेश हृदि स्थितेन
यथा नियुक्तोऽस्मि तथाकरोमि ॥

I know the Law, but have no inclination in me to follow it.

I know what is against the Law, but
have no disinclination for it.
By thee, thou Director of the Senses,
who art seated in my heart,
As I am appointed, so do I act.

Asvini Kumar has not yet reached this stage his *Guru* had. And it is therefore that his very conscientious anxiety to walk in the steps of his *Guru* instead of being a source of strength so frequently becomes a source of weakness in him.

His *Guru* lived absolutely, a life of nature. Now he was as meek as a lamb, and again, if the mood was on him, he became as terrible as a lion. Sometimes he would be tolerant of what to people would seem as the most outrageous of wrongs; at another time he would not stand the least little injustice. Now he was as pliable as clay, and now as hard as adamant. Now crying, now laughing; now exulted, now depressed; now talking the profoundest philosophies, now advising the most irrational things as true and profitable; now an iconoclast of iconoclasts, and the next moment when that impulse had spent itself meekly accepting the current ritualism as good. But all these were natural to him. The Universal himself is a Person of infinite moods, and God himself is the wildest and most irreconcilable of contradictions. These do not hurt the true man of God either. Asvini Kumar's Guru was a man of God. He was a man of many moods like all his class; and in all his moods he stood always absolutely identified, in thinking, feeling and willing—in every department and aspect of his personal life—with the Universal. Such men cannot be measured by any ethical foot-rule. They have their own laws, their own ethics. They are above the Law, because identified with the Law. Who knows what particular course of action Asvini Kumar's *Guru* would have followed in Asvini Kumar's place under any particular circumstance? We examine these circumstances from the outside; and consequently, we interpret frequently their right and wrong not in the light of the Universal scheme in which they stand, but simply according to our own likes and dislikes. Our readings of the circumstances of our life and our duties and obligations to society, are always obscured by the shadow that our own conceit of sense and self casts on them. We do not see them as they really are, in themselves, or as they stand related to the universal scheme of things. But these saints and sages, living in a perpetual consciousness of the Universal, see the passing particularities of life, from the very heart of the Universal; and seeing them all, as part of the Universal order, they deal with every particularity according to its own inner law and purpose. To try to imitate them is not possible for us. We may, if blessed by them, absolutely throw ourselves upon them, and thus live and act from moment to moment, without any preconceived scheme of our own, but just as they move us with their strength and their inspiration which comes to us, not supernaturally, but naturally through the impulses of our flesh, our intellect, our emotions and our will, on the one side, and the outer happenings of our lives, which stimulate these in us, on the other. We may do this. This is the proud privilege of the disciple. But we cannot aspire to follow in their steps, before we have attained their character.

And the desire to do so, seems to me, to be largely responsible for all the indecisions and weaknesses that sometimes his most intimate admirers observe and even regret in Asvini Kumar.

In fact Asvini Kumar is a very fine specimen of the amalgam which is being so numerously manufactured among us, through the combination of Christian and Hindu influences. We are all more or less of the class of this amalgam. Asvini Kumar's inner spirit is essentially Hindu. The meekness, the patience, the absence of restless ambitions, the desire for quiet homely service rather than for tumultuous activities, fidelity to existing social and socio-religious order, even though its passing unreason or ills may be fully recognised, acceptance of duty as a higher principle than right, the spirit of submission rather than of resistance, of forbearance rather than that of revolt, of recrimination—these Hindu characteristics are fairly prominent in Asvini Kumar's life. On the other hand, the keen ethical sense, the passionate longing for the furtherance of social well-being, devotion to public duty and patriotic service, characteristic of the educated European, are also equally prominent features of the life and character of this Bengalee Leader. Asvini Kumar is not a system builder; nor can he lay claim to any original thinking. So he has not been impelled as yet to work out any rational between the Eastern and the Western elements of his composite character. He has not been able to present either the East to himself in the terms of the West, nor to present the West in the terms of the East. The result, therefore, is that sometimes the one element comes out in his thoughts and actions more prominently, and sometimes, the other. Sometimes as an educationist, as a teacher of youth, as an apostle of temperance and purity, as a defender of popular rights against bureaucratic aggressions, Asvini Kumar seems, like so many of us, as fundamentally a handwork of European influences. Sometimes again, especially in the select company of his spiritual friends, while singing the name of the Lord, or reading lessons from the Bhagavata, or discoursing upon BHAKTI-YOGA or KARMA-YOGA,—he seems quite another man, who has more of the old Bhagavata spirit in him than the modern Christian spirit. I have seen him in these select gatherings, and have observed him throwing himself into these ecstatic exercises with an abandonment which one would hardly expect in a man whose whole life and education have been moulded, practically, by Protestant Christian influences.

But it is to the Hindu side of his character that Asvini Kumar owes, I think, his unique position in the public life of his country. As an educationist, as a moral teacher, as a modern public man, devoting himself to the cause of his people and his country, Asvini Kumar could secure a following only among the English-educated classes. In this, he is like the others. And his following even among our English-educated classes, especially in Eastern Bengal, is not insignificant either. I have, indeed, an idea that if a register could be taken of the leaders and workers of the Swadeshi Movement, not only in Barisal, but in all the Eastern districts from Jessore to Mymensing and Sylhet, it would be seen that the largest number by far of them owed their swadeshi inspiration, either directly or indirectly, to Asvini Kumar. Successive generations of University young men from the different districts of Eastern Bengal have flocked to Asvini Kumar's College at Barisal, and have passed under his training and influence the most pregnant and formative periods of their life. And no one who came in contact with him, could escape the influence of his life and conversation. Yet, his position in the history of the present public life of Bengal is so high and absolutely so unique, not because of his literate but because of his illiterate following. And to these it was not the European side of his character that appealed most strongly, but rather his Hindu side.

As a Hindu, Asvini Kumar's type is more Vaishnavic than Shakta. His training is distinctly Vaishnavic. And there is an element of humanity in the Vaishnavic ideal, which is almost modern in both spirit and expression. To see God in man, is the eternal objective of Vaishnavic culture. No other school, I think, has so boldly and openly declared the Godhood of man as the Vaishnavic schools have done. The idealisation of the human flesh as flesh; of the human appetites as appetites; of the varied human relations, as between master and man, or friend and friend, or parent and son, or lover and lover;—to proclaim these as vehicles and instruments of the very life and sport of the Lord,—this is a unique feature of the Vaishnavic ideal and culture. Not the negation or suppression of nature and man, but their idealisation and spiritualisation, through the beatitudes of the soul, is the supreme end of Vaishnavic disciplines. And this Vaishnavic idealism has lent considerable strength and reality to Asvini Kumar's social service.

In the ordinary relations of life, Asvini Kumar observes all the conventions of the Hindu society. But at the call of duty, these conventions fall off from him, like dry autumn leaves. He has not preached against caste, like his early associates in the Brahmo Samaj, but has very materially helped the relaxation of caste-rules in the practical interest of humanity and social service. The students of his school and college have always been trained in the service of the poor and the sick. His volunteers have nursed cholera-patients in times of epidemic, without distinction of caste or creed. Even the women of the town have not been put outside the pale of the service of these devoted youths. And high-caste Brahmins have without the least scruple or hesitancy, cleansed with their own hands the soiled beddings of their low-caste patients, have removed their excreta, and have, when it was found necessary, even carried the dead bodies of the untouchable classes to the burning ghat and cremated these themselves. In times of famine and scarcity, Hindus and Mahomedans have been equally helped by Asvini Kumar and his devoted band. Years of selfless and devoted social service like this, had secured for Asvini Kumar a lasting place in the affections of his people. To them he was never a great and renowned leader, the friend of the Magistrate, and the confidante of the Commissioner,—but their own friend, a present help in their need, an ever-willing guide in their troubles, and a never-failing source of consolation in their sorrows and disappointments. This was the real position of Asvini Kumar among his own neighbours, in his own town and district, long before the birth of the Swadeshi Movement. And it is because of the old influence which he had in the country, that he at once became so powerful a force behind this new movement.

Asvini Kumar's personality is his greatest contribution to the public life of his country and his time. We have had orators, journalists, zemindars, lawyers, medical practitioners, retired high officials, in the leadership of this life. They have done a lot for their country. Some have given us thought, some inspiration, some have paid out of their affluence towards the upkeep of our public propaganda and organisations, and some have added to the weight of our deliberations by their name or their wisdom. But none, except Asvini Kumar Datta, has given us the exact pattern after which the true leader must be made henceforth.

Asvini Kumar's personality is the greatest force in Barisal. And this has been so, because he has always been one of the people, one with them in thought and life. In the future, the real leadership of the public life everywhere will be based upon this close, this personal relation between the leader and his following. Not the man with the longest purse, nor the man with the most powerful tongue, nor he with the ripest wisdom, will be acclaimed as its leader by modern democracy, but only he who, whatever his wealth, or education or wisdom, will be one with his people and whose people will be one with him—will be the true leader of men. In Asvini Kumar we have a glimpse of this coming type. But after all, the type is not altogether new either. It is the old, old type, coming back to us, revivified and modernised,—that is all.

ARAVINDA GHOSE

The youngest in age among those who stand in the forefront of the Nationalist propaganda in India, but in endowment, education, and character, perhaps, superior to them all—Aravinda seems distinctly marked out by Providence to play in the future of this movement a part not given to any of his colleagues and contemporaries. The other leaders of the movement have left their life behind them: Aravinda has his before him. Nationalism is their last love: it is Aravinda's first passion. They are burdened with the cares and responsibilities of large families or complex relations: Aravinda has a small family and practically no cumulative obligations. His only care is for his country—the mother, as he always calls her. His only recognised obligations are to her. Nationalism, at the best, a concern of the intellect with some, at the lowest a political cry and aspirations with others, is with Aravinda a supreme passion of his soul. Few, indeed, have grasped the full force and meaning of the Nationalist ideal as Aravinda has done. But even of these very few—though their vision may be clear, their action is weak. Man cannot, by a fiat of his will at once recreate his life. Our Karma follows us with relentless insistence from day to day and from death to death. To see the vision of truth and yet not to be possessed by the supreme passion for it which burns up all other desires and snaps asunder, like ashen bands, all other ties and obligations—this is the divine tragedy of most finer natures. They have to cry out with St. Paul at every turn of life's tortuous path—"The Spirit is willing, but the flesh is weak." But blessed are they for whom this tragic antithesis between the ideal and the real has been cancelled: for whom to know the truth is to love it, to love the truth is to strive after it, and to strive after the truth is to attain it: in whom there is no disparity, either in time or degree, between the idea and its realisation: in whom the vision of the ideal, by its own intrinsic strength at once attunes every craving of the flesh, every movement of the mind, every motion of the heart, and every impulse of the will to itself: who have to strive for its realisation, not within, but without: who have to struggle not with their own Self, but with the Not-Self : who have to fight and conquer not themselves but others, in order to establish the kingdom of God, realised by them in the relations of their own inner life, in the actualities and appointments of the life of their own people or of humanity at large. These are, so to say, the chosen of God. They are born leaders of men. Commissioned to serve special ends affecting the life and happiness of large masses of men, they bear a charmed life. They may be hit, but cannot be hurt. They may be struck, but are never stricken. Their towering optimism, and the Grace of God, turn every evil into good, every opposition into help, every loss into a gain. By the general verdict of his countrymen, Aravinda stands to-day among these favoured sons of God.

Birth is not an accident. "Accident of birth"—is the language of infidel empiricism. Nature has no room for accidents in her schemes. It is only man's inability to trace her secrets that has coined this word to cover his ignorance. Man's birth is no more an accident than the rise and fall of tides. There can really be no accidents in evolution; the law of natural selection has killed their chance altogether. But does the operation of natural selection start only after the birth of the organism or does it precede it? Is it only a biological, or also a psychological law? Like the problems of biology, those of psychology also are inexplicable, except on this theory. The inference is irresistible that there is such a thing as natural selection even in the psychic plane. The spirit, by the impulse of its own needs must choose and order the conditions of its life even as the physical organism does. This is the psychic significance of heredity. Life from this point of view is not a lottery, but a matter really of determined choice. The needs of the organism supply the organs in the lower kingdom: the desires of the heart collect and create the necessary equipment and environment for the human being. On no other hypothesis can the riddle of the human life be explained more satisfactorily. It may not explain everything, but it explains many things absolutely ununderstandable and inexplicable on any other hypothesis. This at least has been the Hindu view from time immemorial. A crude intuition at first, it became a settled conviction with the people subsequently, with a fundamental philosophy of causation behind it. And this theory stands curiously verified in Aravinda Ghose.

Two strong currents of thoughts, ideals, and aspirations met together and strove for supremacy in Bengal, among the generation to which Aravinda's parents belonged. One was a current of Hindu Nationalism—of the revived life, culture and ideals of the nation that had lain dormant for centuries and had been discarded as lower and primitive by the first batch of English-educated Hindus, specially in Bengal. The other was the current of Indo-Anglicism—the onrushing life, culture and ideals of the foreign rulers of the land, which, expressing themselves through British law and administration on the one side, and the new schools and universities on the other, threatened to swamp and drown the original culture and character of the people. The two stocks from which Aravinda sprang represented these two conflicting forces in the country. His maternal grandfather, Raj Narain Bose was one of the makers of modern Bengal. A student of David Hare, a pupil of De Rozario, an alumnus of the Hindu College, the first English college that had the support of both the Hindu community and the British rulers of the Province, Raj Narain Bose started life as a social and religious reformer. But while he caught as fully as any one else among his contemporaries, the impulse of the new illumination, he did not lose so completely as many of them did, his hold on the fundamental spirit of the culture and civilisation of his race. He joined the Brahmo Samaj, under Maharshi Debendra Nath Tagore, but felt repelled by the denational spirit of the later developments in that movement under Keshub Chunder Sen. In fact, it is difficult to say, to which of its two leaders—Debendra Nath or Raj Narain, the Adi or the older Brahmo-Samaj, as it came to be called after Keshub Chunder Sen seceded from it and established the Brahmo-Samaj of India—was more indebted for its intense and conservative nationalism. But it may be safely asserted that while Debendra Nath's nationalism had a dominating theological note, Raj Narain's had both a theological and social, as well as a political emphasis. In him it was not merely the spirit of Hinduism that rose up in arms against the onslaught of European Christianity, but the whole spirit of Indian culture and manhood stood up to defend and assert itself against every form of undue foreign influence and alien domination. While Keshub Chunder Sen pleaded for the recognition of the truths in the Hindu scriptures side by side with those in the Bible, Raj Narain Bose proclaimed the superiority of Hinduism to Christianity. While Keshub Chunder was seeking to reconstruct Indian, and especially Hindu, social life, more or less after the British model, Raj Narain's sturdy patriotism and national self-respect rebelled against the enormity, and came forward to establish the superiority of Hindu social economy to the Christian social institutions and ideals. He saw the on-rush of European goods into Indian markets, and tried to stem the tide by quickening what we would now call the Swadeshi spirit, long before any one else had thought of it. It was under his inspiration that a Hindu Mela or National Exhibition was started a full quarter of a century before the Indian National Congress thought of an Indian Industrial Exhibition. The founder of this Hindu Mela was also the first Bengalee who organised gymnasia for the physical training of the youths of the nation. Stick and sword plays, and other ancient but decadent sports and pastimes of the people that have come into vogue recently, were originally revived at the Hindu Mela under Raj Narayan Bose's inspiration and instruction. Raj Narayan Bose did not openly take any part in politics, but his writings and speeches did a good deal to create that spirit of self-respect and self-assertion in the educated classes that have since found such strong expression in our recent political activities.

A strong conservatism, based upon a

reasoned appreciation of the lofty spirituality of the ancient culture and civilisation of the country; a sensitive patriotism, born of a healthy and dignified pride of race; and a deep piety expressing itself through all the varied practical relations of life—these were the characteristics of the life and thought of Raj Narayan Bose. He represented the high-water-mark of the composite culture of his country—Vedantic, Islamic, and European. When he discoursed on Brahma-Jnan or knowledge of God, he brought to mind the ancient Hindu gnostics of the Upanishads. When he cited verses from the Persian poets, filling the ear with their rich cadence—with his eyes melting in love and his mobile features aglow with a supreme spiritual passion—he reminded one of the old Moslem devotees. And when he spoke on the corruptions of current religion, or the soulless selfishness of modern politics, he appeared as a nineteenth century nationalist and iconoclast of Europe. In his mind and life he was at once a Hindu Maharshi, a Moslem Shafi, and a Christian theist of the Unitarian type; and like Ram Mohan

Roy, the founder of the Brahmo-Samaj of which Raj Narayan Bose was for many years the honoured president, he also seems to have worked out a synthesis in his own spiritual life between the three dominant world-cultures that have come face to face in modern India. Like Ram Mohan, Raj Narayan also seems to have realised himself, intellectually and spiritually, that ideal of composite nationhood in India, which the present generation has been called upon to actualise in social, economic and political relations of their country. Raj Narayan Bose was also an acknowledged leader in Bengali literature. A writer in the "Modern Review" (Calcutta) calls Raj Narayan Bose "The Grandfather of Indian Nationalism." He was Aravinda's maternal grandfather; and Aravinda owes not only his rich spiritual nature but even his very superior literary capacity to his inherited endowments from his mother's line.

If his maternal grandfather represented the ancient spiritual forces of his nation, Aravinda's father, Dr. Krista Dhan Ghose, represented to a very large extent the spirit of the new illumination in his country. Dr. Ghose was essentially a product of English education and European culture. A man of exceptional parts, he finished his education in England and taking his degree in medicine, entered the medical service of the Indian Government. He was one of the most successful Civil Surgeons of his day, and, had his life been spared, he would have assuredly risen to the highest position in his service open to any native of India. Like the general body of Indian young men who came to finish their education in England in his time, Krista Dhan Ghose was steeped in the prevailing spirit of Anglicism. Like all of them he was a thoroughly Anglicised Bengalee, in his ways of life. But unlike many of them, underneath his foreign clothing and ways he had a genuine Hindu heart and soul. Anglicism distorts Hindu character, cripples, where it cannot kill, the inherited altruism of the man, and makes him more or less neglectful of the numerous family and social obligations under which every Hindu is born. Like the original Anglo-Saxon, his Indian imitation also lives first and foremost for himself, his wife and children ; and though he may recognise the claims of his relations to his charity, he scarcely places his purse at their service as an obligation. But Krista Dhan Ghose was an exception. Though he affected the European ways of living, he never neglected the social obligation of the Hindu. His purse was always open for his needy relations.

The poor of the town, where he served and lived, had in him a true friend and a ready help. In fact, his regard for the poor frequently led him to sacrifice to their present needs the future prospects of his own family and children. He had his sons educated in England; and so great was his admiration for English life and English culture that he sent them out here even before they had received any schooling in their country. But his charities met such constant and heavy inroads into his tolerably large income that he could not always keep his own children living in England provided with sufficient funds for their board and schooling. Sons of comparatively rich parents they were brought up almost in abject poverty in a friendless country where wealth counts so much, not only physically, but also intellectually and morally. Keen of intellect, tender of heart, impulsive and generous almost to recklessness regardless of his own ones, but sensitive to the sufferings of others—this was the inventory of the character of Dr. Krista Dhan Ghose. The rich blamed him for his recklessness, the man of the world condemned him for his absolute lack of prudence, the highest virtue in his estimation. But the poor, the widow and the orphan loved him for his selfless pity, and his soulful benevolence.

When death overtook him in the very prime of life there was desolation in many a poor home in his district. It not only left his own children in absolute poverty, but destroyed the source of ready relief to many helpless families among his relations and neighbours. His quick intellectual perception, his large sympathies, his selflessness, characterised by an almost absolute lack of what the man of the world always working with an eye to the main chance, calls prudence, as a matter of personal calculation,—these are Aravinda's inheritance in his father's line.

As a boy, Aravinda received his early education in a public school in England. The old Head Master of this school is reported to have said, when Aravinda's name came prominently before the British public in connection with the state trial of which he was made a principal accused, this time last year, that of all the boys who passed through his hands during the last twenty-five or thirty years, Aravinda was by far and above the most richly endowed in intellectual capacity. From this school he went to Cambridge, where he distinguished himself as a student of European classics, and passed the Indian Civil Service examination with great credit. Failing, however, to stand the required test in horsemanship, he was not allowed to enter the covenanted service of the Indian Government. But returning to India, he found employment in the native state of Baroda, where his endowments and scholarship soon attracted the notice of authorities, leading to his appointment to the post of Vice-Principal of the State College. Had Aravinda cared for earthly honours or wealth, he had a very splendid opening for both in Baroda. He was held in great respect by the Maharaja. He was loved by the educated classes in the State. He was exceedingly popular with the general public. All these opened very large possibilities of preferment before him in the service of the premier Native State in India.

But there was a new awakening in the country. A new school of thought had arisen, demanding a thorough reconsideration of the old and popular political, economic, and educational ideas and ideals of the people. It abjured the old mendicant methods of prayer, protest and petition. It proclaimed a new gospel of self-help and self-reliance. It called out to the spirit of India to come to its own, to stand upon its own inner strength, and to put forth its native efforts for the realisation of its true native life. It called aloud for leaders and workers—for the poet, the prophet, the philosopher, the statesman, the organiser and the man of action, to help the sacred cause. It laid on all who would accept the call the heaviest self-sacrifice yet demanded of any public man in modern India. It wanted men who would not only, as hitherto, give to their country their leisure moments and their idle pennies, but who would consecrate all their working hours and their hard earnings to the service of the Motherland. The call went to the heart of Aravinda. His own native Province called for him. It laid on him the vow of poverty. It offered him the yoke of the saviours of their people and the uplifters of humanity—the yoke of calumny, persecution, imprisonment and exile. Aravinda obeyed the Mother's call, accepted her stern conditions, and cheerfully took up her chastening yoke. He gave up his place in Baroda, worth £560 a year, to take up the duties of Principal in the College started at Calcutta under the new National Council of Education on a bare subsistence allowance of £10 a month.

This movement of national education owed its origin to the latest education-policy of the Indian Government, who sought to turn the institutions of public instruction in the country to distinctly political ends. The old education had given birth to widespread disaffection. It called into being "the discontented B.A. s." The new educational policy initiated by Lord Curzon was directed towards curing this evil. Its aim was to manufacture loyal citizens—men who would be eternally content to remain loyal to the autocratic government in their country, without any desire for free citizenship. The movement of National Education was the people's reply to this official policy. It took definite shape and form as a result of the persecution of schoolboys, by the Executive in Bengal, for their participation in the new political movements in the country. But it had a more fundamental need. The officially-controlled education had been condemned by both friends and foes alike. It was shallow and rootless. It imparted the shadow, but not the substance, of modern culture to the youths of the nation. It was artificial, because foreign in both spirit and form. It led to a fearful waste of youthful time and energy by imposing the necessity of learning a foreign language, to receive instructions through its medium in all higher branches of study. Its was controlled by an alien

Bureaucracy, in the interest, mainly, of their own political position, and only secondarily in those of real intellectual life of the pupils. It was excessively literary, and detrimental to the industrial and economical life of the country. The movement of National Education was started to counteract these evils of the officially controlled system of public instruction. It proposed to promote—"Education, scientific, literary, and technical, on national lines and under national control." But though owing its initiation to the threats of the Government to close the doors of the official schools, colleges and universities against those who would take any part—even to the extent of simply attending--in any political meeting or demonstration—the National Education Movement in Bengal sought to avoid all open causes of friction with the authorities, and professed to work *independent of* but not in *opposition* to the Government. Political in its origin, it tried to avoid all conflicts with the authorities by assuming an absolutely non-political attitude.

The school of thought to which Aravinda belonged did not support this declaration of the National Council of Education and could not appreciate this needless dread, as they thought, of offending official susceptibilities. But they had to accept the verdict of the majority. One of the most unfortunate things in modern public life is the dependence of all large public movement on the help and support of the wealthy classes in the community. Large and organised movements in our time cannot be carried on without large and substantial financial support; and the rich are not willing, as they were in the primitive times, to lend their support to any institution without seeking to control it. This unfortunate condition lowers the intellectual and moral tone of many a public institution which though financed with the monies of the richer classes, would have been able without their personal intervention or control, to keep up a very superior intellectual or moral standard. This is particularly injurious in comparitively primitive communities, where realised wealth has not yet had time to ally itself with high culture, and where, owing to the absence of a vigorous and free national life, it has but little incentive and lesser opportunity for cultivating such an alliance.

The Nationalists are a poor party in India, and the National Council of Education, though it owed its initiation to their efforts passed, almost from the very beginning, beyond their sphere of influence, and Aravinda's position as the nominal head of the National College, practically controlled by men of different views and opinions, became almost from the very beginning more or less anomalous.

This was, from some point of view, very unfortunate. Aravinda had received the best modern education that any man of his country and generation could expect to have. He had for some years been a teacher of youth in Baroda, and had acquired considerable practical experience in his art. He had clearly realised the spirit and actualities of the life of his nation, and knew how the most advanced principles of modern pedagogy could be successfully worked into a thoroughly national system of education in India. He went to Calcutta as an educationist. He knew that the foundations of national independence and national greatness must be laid in a strong and advanced system of national education. He had a political ideal, no doubt; but politics meant to him much more than is ordinarily understood by the term. It was not a game of expediency, but a school of human character, and, in his turn, reacting upon it, should develop and strengthen the manhood and woomanhood of the nation.. Education could no more be divorced from politics than it could be divorced from religion or morals. Any system of education that helps such isolaation and division between the various organic relations of life, is mediæval, and not modern. It is the education of the cloister—abstract and unreal; not the education of the modern man, eager to realise his fullest manhood in and through every relation of life. Aravinda is an apostle of modern education. Indeed, his ideal of modern education is even higher than what is understood by modern education ordinarily in Europe. It is a supremely spiritual ideal. Its aim is to actualise the highest and deepest God-consciousness of the human soul, in the outer life and appointments of human society. It was a temptation of having an open field for the realisation of this lofty educational ideal which brought Aravinda to Calcutta. Had he been given a free hand in the new National College there, that institution would have opened an altogether new chapter not only in the history of modern education in India, but perhaps in the whole world. To work the realism of the spirit of modern culture into the mould of the idealism of ancient philosophy, would not only secure for India her lost position as teacher of humanity, but would, perchance, even save modern civilisation from total collapse and destruction under the pressure of a gross and greedy industrialism.

But, unfortunately, neither individuals nor communities can easily break away from their own past. Most of the members of the new National Council of Education in Bengal were products of the old university. Some of the leading men of the new organisation had been closely associated, for many years, with the actual working out of the old vicious system.

Steeped in the traditions of this old education, they could hardly be expected to thoroughly enter into the spirit of modern pedagogy. They were willing to give fair room to the new principles, as an experiment, but could hardly give them their absolute and whole-hearted support as truths. It seemed to them like jumping into the unknown. While accepting the principle of national education as education on national lines and under national control, and, consequently, pledged not to accept any official aid, they were not free from the fear of possible official opposition, which, if once aroused, would make their work, they thought, absolutely impossible. They had a real dread of the Bureaucracy, and no strong confidence, really, in their own people. The dominating and declared ideal of the new Council, consequently, came to be not in any way to supplant, but only to supplement, the existing Government-and-University-system of education in the country. A timid, temporizing spirit, so galling to the reformer and the man with new visions and large ideas, generally guided the work of the National Council, and it made it almost impossible for Aravinda to throw himself heart and soul into his educational work in Calcutta. His place in the National College, though he was its nominal Principal, was not really that of an organiser and initiator, but simply of a teacher of language and history, even as it had been in the Maharaja's College at Baroda. He had left Baroda in the hope of finding a wider scope of beneficient and patriotic activity in the new College in Calcutta. That hope was not realised. Almost from the very beginning he saw the hopelessness of working out a truly modern and thoroughly national system of education, through the organisation at whose service he had so enthusiastically placed himself.

But the man possessed by pure passion, creates, where he cannot find them ready-made for him, his own instruments for the realisation of his supreme end in life. And wider fields of public usefulness were soon opened before Aravinda. The National School was without a daily English Organ. A new paper was started. Aravinda was invited to join its staff. A joint-stock company was shortly floated to run it, and Aravinda became one of the directors. This paper—"Bande Mataram"—at once secured for itself a recognised position in Indian journalism. The hand of the master was in it, from the very beginning. Its bold attitude, its vigorous thinking, its clear ideas, its chaste and powerful diction, its scorching sarcasm and refined witticism, were unsurpassed by any journal in the country, either Indian or Anglo-Indian. It at once raised the tone of every Bengali paper, and compelled the admiration of even hostile Anglo-Indian editors. Morning after morning, not only Calcutta but the educated community almost in every part of the country, eagerly awaited its vigorous pronouncements on the stirring questions of the day. It even forced itself upon the notice of the callous and self-centred British press. Long extracts from it commenced to be reproduced week after week even in the exclusive columns of the "Times" in London. It was a force in the country which none dared to ignore, however much they might fear or hate it, and Aravinda was the leading spirit, the central figure, in the new journal. The opportunities that were denied him in the National College he found in the pages of the "Bande Mataram," and from a tutor of a few youths he thus became the teacher of a whole nation.

SRIJUT KRISHNA KUMAR MITRA

Srijut Krishna Kumar Mitra does not belong to what is called the Nationalist Party in India, but he is undoubtedly a prominent man in the Nationalist Movement. The Nationalist Movement is much larger than the Nationalist party. This party is a much later growth than the movement of which it has commenced to take a lead. The Nationalist or the Extremist party, as it is called by its opponents, is hardly three years old, and even now it can hardly be called a party. It is more a school of thought than an organised and disciplined political party. Before 1906 there was only one National Party in India and that was the Congress party. It was only in the autumn of that year when an attempt was made to secure the nomination of Srijut Bal Gangadhar Tilak to the Congress Presidency, that Congressmen all over the country divided themselves into two camps, one being called Moderates and the other Extremists. These names were not of their own choosing. They were invented and given to them by their common enemies of the Anglo-Indian Press. In Bengal, at any rate, both the schools disclaimed the names thus given to them, and claimed to be equally Nationalists. There has, in fact, been much less fundamental divergencies of views between these two schools in Bengal than in any other Indian province. In Bengal, the so-called Moderates and the so-called Extremists have been united in the fundamental and positive methods of the Nationalist Movement. The Bengalee "Moderate" until the closing weeks of the last year, had been a staunch advocate of Swadeshi and Boycott, National Education, and National Volunteering. The only points of difference between the two schools have been—(i) in regard to the ideal, and (ii) in regard to the scope of the Boycott. The Bengalee Moderates proclaimed Colonial Self-Government as their ideal instead of the absolute autonomy set up as the ultimate goal by the so-called Extremists, and unlike the latter, they refused to extend the Boycott to all voluntary offices under the Government.

To work in association with the Government wherever such association is likely to be useful and beneficial to the country, and in opposition to them, when it is necessary in the public interest—this has been the avowed policy of the Bengalee "Moderates." In this they stood apart from the so-called Extremists, who advocated an absolute dissociation from all official connections and obligations, except where they were absolutely enjoined by law. But whether "Moderates" or "Extremists" every, or almost every, Bengalee public man belongs to the larger movement of Nationalism in India, whose one cry is "India for the Indians."

To this class belongs Srijut Krishna Kumar Mitra. Like his friend and leader Srijut Surendra Nath Banerjee, Krishna Kumar has been one of the forces of Nationalism in Bengal. Indeed, we know it as a matter of fact, that he has strongly repudiated this division of the people into rival political parties and urged always for united action. This is what he persistently preached in his paper, "The Sanjibani," which was at one time the real mouthpiece of English-educated Bengalees, especially of the eastern districts, where it had enormous influence. And if Krishna Kumar did find himself occasionally in open opposition to the so-called Extremists of Bengal, it was due not so much to vital difference of principle between them and himself, as to his personal love and regard for Babu Surendra Nath Banerjee, with whom he had worked all his life. Had not some of the Bengalee Extremists openly repudiated the leadership of Babu Surendra Nath, Krishna Kumar would have been as much in association and sympathy with them as with the so-called Bengalee Moderates. But Moderate or Extremist, every prominent public man in Bengal has been and is a Nationalist. Bengal has not yet known the type represented by Pherozeshah Mehta or Gopal Krishna Gokhale in Bombay. And Krishna Kumar is by no means of that type.

And the chief reason of it is that Krishna Kumar is not a politician in the ordinary sense of the term. If Aswini Kumar approaches the type of the Hindu devotee, Krishna Kumar approaches that of the Hebrew prophet. In fact, both by temperament and training, Krishna Kumar is what may be called more Semitic and Christian than Hindu and Vaishnava. He belongs to a generation that had completely lost touch with the inner spirit and ancient traditions of their race. In early life he imbibed the spirit of religious and social revolt headed by Keshub Chunder Sen. The Brahmo Samaj or the Theistic Church of India under Keshub Chunder Sen in his earlier days, was in its tone and temper distinctly more Hebraic than Hindu. The thought-leaders of the Brahmo Samaj in those days were Theodore Parker and Francis Newman and Miss Frances Power Cobbe on the theological and ethical side, and Victor Cousin and the Scotch Intuitionalists on the speculative and philosophical side. The mind and spirit of Keshub Chunder and his followers fed on these teachings, and he himself represented at that time more the prophetic fervour of Hebrew theism than the transcendental depth or the devotional sweetness of Hindu Monism and Vaishnavic piety. Keshub Chunder gradually grew, later in life, into these national ideals no doubt, and he died more a Hindu than a Hebrew or a Christian in his spirit and aspirations. But Krishna Kumar had cut himself off from his leadership before these later phases of thought and devotion developed in the great Brahmo leader and has persistently kept up the earlier inspiration he had imbibed from him.

The Brahmo Samaj, under Keshub Chunder Sen, represented both the fruit of, and the earliest reaction against, the impact of the Hindu mind with the dominating thought and culture of modern Europe. It was not only the child of this new illumination but also, at the same time, represented the earliest protest of the Hindu spirit against being completely dominated by it. In both these aspects it was essentially a movement of freedom. It proclaimed the divine authority of human reason in the determination of truth, and openly discarded the time-honoured pretensions of religious scriptures to special and supernatural revelation. It acknowledged no prophets, accepted no priests, but set each individual free to seek and find the truth for himself or herself, and directly approach the

Throne of Grace with his or her own prayers and aspirations, these aspirations of the devout spirit of man or woman finding their response and fulfilment in inspiration from God, and thus completing the highest process of spiritual and devotional exercises, and directly leading to the soul's salvation. This gospel of personal freedom naturally led to a movement of social reform which aimed at a thorough reconstruction of Indian, and practically of Hindu domestic and social life, after the new ideal. Child marriages and non-consensual marriages were discarded as an usurpation of personal rights in a matter of the greatest concern to the peace and happiness of the individual. The disabilities of Hindu widows in regard to remarriages were openly removed for the same reason. Distinctions of caste, not only in the matter of eating and drinking, but also in the matter of marital relations, were completely discarded as immoral and injurious. The rights of the human personality to freely realise itself with outlet or hindrance from undue social interference or sacerdotal or religious restraints, were proclaimed thus, in every direction.

The Brahmo Samaj was, thus, a movement of freedom. In the days of his youth, when Krishna Kumar came under its influence, the Brahmo Samaj was essentially individualistic in its conceptions of personal rights and in its general philosophy of human freedom. It was, in some sense, the child of the European Illumination of the eighteenth century and had the excessive individualistic emphasis of that great movement of protest. The genius of Kehsub Chunder Sen, however, soon recognised the limits of individualism, and he spent the last years of his life in devising a variety of means to correct and cure the evils of this excessive individualistic emphasis. To find a legitimate ground and sanction for individual impulses and notions, he fell back upon what was called the doctrine of individual inspiration. To correct the confusion and conflict arising out of the claim of each individual to direct divine inspiration, Keshub Chunder Sen fell back upon the Catholic doctrine of the Church as the ever-present instrument of communication between God and man, and set up the Council of the Apostles of the new creed, called Sree Darbar, as an objective authority for the regulation and guidance of individual inspiration. The injurious tendencies of the individualism of the later eighteenth and the earlier nineteenth centuries were manifested in three directions—in theology it developed athesim and scepticism; in social life it developed license and immorality; in politics it developed revolutionary anarchism. Keshub Chunder Sen soon recognised these tendencies, and was frightened by their apparition into taking refuge in a conservative creed, which he proclaimed as the fundamental creed of his Church. This creed was summed up in the three-fold loyalty (i) to God, (ii) to Church, and (iii) to King. By means of this three-fold loyalty he tried to harmonise the movement of progress with the cause of order and work out a reconciliation between authority and independence.

But Krishna Kumar having seceded from the leading of Keshub Chunder Sen before these developments, had absolutely no participation in them. His religious and social ideals have always continued to be those of the early days of the Brahmo Samaj. But his superior moral nature has always saved him from the logical excesses of his essentially individualistic philosophy. Ever since his youth Krishna Kumar has accepted and proclaimed the authority of individual reason as the ultimate judge of truth and that of individual conscience as the final arbiter of right and wrong; but he has never, in practical life, identified opinion with truth or mixed up personal impulses with the promptings of conscience. Krishna Kumar has, therefore, been a reformer, but not a revolutionary in any sense of the term.

Constitutionally free from the extremely speculative tendencies of his race, Krishna Kumar has tenaciously clung to the simple faith of his youth. Though by no means incapable of very strong emotions, the type of piety which Krishna Kumar represents is decidedly more Semitic and volitional than Vaishnavic and emotional. His conscience has therefore been the main controlling force of his life. The voice of conscience has always been to him the very voice of his God. In his loyalty to conscience Krishna Kumar represents among us that stern Puritan type of virile personality which woked up the Rebellion in England and founded a Republic in America.

Krishna Kumar is incapable of deliberately doing a thing which he believes to be wrong. But once convinced of the truth or justice of the cause he will fight for it to the bitterest end, and will never shrink from making any sacrifice, however great, to serve it. Without the least suspicion of bravado, he has been the most fearless of our public men. At Barisal in 1906, when the police charged a peaceful procession of delegates to the Bengal Provincial Conference with their quarter-staff, and were innocently breaking some heads in the discharge of their duty as guardians of peace and protectors of the people, Krishna Kumar was the only man who rushed between the unarmed and helpless delegates and their assailants, repelled an assaulting constable with his umbrella, dragged him to the Superintendent of Police, under whose evident instructions these assaults were being made, and literally ordered that officer to stop these illegal excesses; and the moral fervour of the man so completely cowed down that officer that he at once called back his men, and further assaults were stopped. Had the occasion demanded and his conscience prompted him, Krishna Kumar could have faced a cannon's mouth with as much unconcern as that with which he rushed here between a pack of police hooligans and their helpless victims. When the order of the Magistrate of Barisal was brought to the Conference demanding its immediate breaking up, and armed policemen with fixed bayonets were walking up and down the street, waiting for a signal from the Superintendent to charge that peaceful gathering of absolutely unarmed men and women, Krishna Kumar was the only prominent man on the platform who refused to move out in submission to an unjust and illegal order. It was his duty to resist every wrong and he would resist this wrong also, utterly regardless of whatever might happen either to himself or even to the hunderds of ladies and even children who had come to the meeting with their elders. When it is a question of duty, no prudential considerations of any kind find any place in the thoughts of this man of conscience.

The Brahmo Samaj, of which Krishna Kumar has been a leader and minister for many years past professes a very simple creed, and is guided by a very simple philosophy of life. It believes in God, in the duty of worship, the efficiency of prayer, and in the existence of a future life. It refuses to accept any authority in matters of faith, except that of man's own reason and conscience, and repudiates all incarnations and mediations. Man's relations with his Maker are immediate and personal. It proclaims the Fatherhood of God and the Brotherhood of man. Its code of duty is summed up in the worship of God and the pursuit of objects that are pleasing to Him. Love of God and the service of man constitute all the rites and sacraments of this simple creed. And this simple creed and philosophy of life and this code of duty contain the entire inventory of the life and character of Krishna Kumar. His activities, whether as a teacher of youth, or as a social reformer or political worker, or as a preacher of religion, have all been prompted and guided by this simple creed and philosophy. Social and political reforms, as calculated to improve human character, remove human misery and promote love and justice among men, are supreme demands in Krishna Kumar's religion. His patriotism is only an expression of his piety. But though the sincerity and strength of his devotion to his Motherland stand as high as that of any of our public men, in one sense Krishna Kumar is much less of a Nationalist than perhaps most of them. Nationalism as a philosophy of life and as a necessary element in the evolution of universal humanity, has found as yet no place, I am afraid, in Krishna Kumar's general scheme of thought. The prevailing and popular social philosophy of the Brahmo Samaj has so far been more pronounced on the cosmopolitan than on the national side. As in Brahmo theology nothing mediates between the individual and the Universal, so in Brahmo sociology nothing stands as a medium of relation or realisation, between individual man and universal humanity. The organic conception of society and the general, social philosophy that is rapidly growing out in our age, have not as yet been able to powerfully influence the social ideals of the Brahmo Samaj as a body. Consequently, this community has not been able as yet to receive the inspiration of what may be called rational and philosophic nationalism. On the other hand being essentially a movement of protest and reform, and as such, constantly emphasising the evil and unreason of the old social order and the traditional social ideal and the religious beliefs of the people, it has lost the advantage of that natural conservatism which finds the motif of nationalism among the general unthinking populace everywhere. Few Brahmos can, therefore, be real Nationalists in either sense of the term; and Krishna Kumar is not, in any way, identified with this few. An abstract cosmopolitanism is the dominating principle of the social philosophy which he has in common with the orthodox section of his own denomination. Krishna Kumar is, therefore, free from that persistent and almost constitutional antipathy against the foreigner that so frequently forms such an ugly feature of nationalism and patriotism all the world over. His patriotism is essentially an expression of his general humanity. The inspiration of his political activities as much as that of his social revolt, comes from his inherent love of justice and hatred of wrong more than from any special and passionate love for his people, as his own people, and standing apart from the other peoples of the world. He would fight as strenuously for redressing the wrongs of the Hottentot as he has been doing for the emancipation of the Hindu. Krishna Kumar is one of the few Indian Public men who can say, in the words of the English poet :—

I live for those that love me,
For those that know me true,
For the Heaven that smiles above me,
And waits my coming too.

* * * *

For every cause that lacks assistance,
For every cause that needs resistance,
The future in the distance,
And the good that I can do.

SRIJUT SYAM SUNDAR CHAKRAVARTI

Srijut Syam Sundar Chakravarti, before his deportation last December, was known outside Bengal, mainly through his connection with the *Bande Mataram* newspaper. He was present at the Congress that failed at Surat, where his simplicity of life and habits, his steadfast devotion to the Nationalist cause, his uncompromising regard for the ideals and principles that stand for Nationalism in India, won him the admiration and love of the large body of Nationalists gathered from all parts of the country. Henceforth he came to be regarded as one of the leaders of the movement on the Bengal side.

In his own province, however, Syam Sundar has been long known as a very capable Bengali journalist and writer. His paper the *Pratibasi* occupied the foremost place among Bengali weeklies, in regard to its thoughtfulness, sobriety, and superior literary character. But popular and sensational journalism has, to a very large extent, destroyed the chances of success of high class literary journals in Bengal, as elsewhere; and the *Pratibasi* succumbed after a few years to the severe financial strain under which it lived and laboured almost all through its life. When the *Sandhya* was started by the late Brahmo Bandhab Upadhyaya, Syam Sundar joined its staff, and his simple and racy style contributed very largely to the unique success which that paper attained at one part of its life. When the *Bande Mataram* was organised as a joint stock concern, about the end of 1906, Syam Sundar left the *Sandhya* and joined its staff, and he was, to a very large extent, the very life and soul of that paper, until it was suppressed by the Government last November. A few weeks later, Syam Sundar was himself arrested and deported under Regulation III of 1818 without any public indictment or trial.

Syam Sundar belongs to a generation that came very largely under the influence of the Hindu Revival of the closing quarter of the last century. Unlike Aswini Kumar, Krishna Kumar, or Manoranjan,

—Syam Sundar had never broken away from the ancient thoughts and traditions of his people, and, consequently, while Aswini Kumar and Manoranjan represent what may be called the return movement in Bengali thought and ife of our time, Syam Sundar represents the type of staunch nationalism that comes through the natural and instinctive conservatism of every people. He has, of course, come under the rationalistic influence of his age, and has had, therefore, to work out some sort of synthesis between old ideas and institutions on the one side, and the new thoughts, aspirations, and conditions on the other. But he did not come through any open antithesis or protest but grew naturally, and almost unconsciously through the normal evolution of his intellectual and social environments.

No revival can really revive the past, just as it was in the past. It has to adjust the past to the living conditions of the present. A successful revival must, therefore, offer a new view-point and a new synthesis. It is in such a synthesis that the Hindu Revival in India of the last quarter of a century has had its main strength. And it must be admitted that the underlying thought of this Revival has more or less operly and consciously taken note of the protest of reason raised by the Brahmo Samaj and other religious reform movements of our day.

Neo-Hindusim, as it is called, is not really the Hindusim of our fathers; it is a new phase, a new development, a new interpretation, and a new adjusment of the old and traditional ideals, in the light of present needs and conditions. Every reaction means, as Emerson says, the halt of reason and its movement backward to pick up some neglected truth that had been previously lost sight of and left on the way. The movements of protest, inaugurated under alien influences, had left many a precious truth behind. They had ever emphasised the unreason and injustice of ancient thoughts and institutions, and had therefore overlooked the soul of truth and the counterpoise of good that lie mixed up everywhere with falsehoods and evils. Those movements were more or less forced from the outside, through the influence of imported ideas and ideals, and these latter brought in their train their own necessary counterpoise of falsehoods and evils, which being foreign to the thought and life of the people, met with no natural antidote that society almost unconsciously and automatically always and everywhere provides against the necessary evils of its own native life and thought. All these combined to contribute to the strength of the reaction which passed over the country during the closing decades of the last century. It obstructed the advance of the aggressive religious and social reform movements visibly; but all the same, contributed to the general progress of thought and life, almost in every direction. The present Nationalist Movement in India is very largely indebted to this Reaction or Revival for a good deal both of its inner strength and its outer influence.

Syam Sunder is essentially a child of this Reaction. He has always clung to the spirit and traditions of his race with a tender tenacity, that, while recognising their frailties, yet shrank from ruthlessly rooting them up lest the sacred organism itself should be wounded and injured in the operation. But he has also been sensitive to liberal influences, and has been sincerely respectful to the the leaders of the Brahmo Samaj and other reform movements; but being essentially a man of sentiment he has never permitted his intellectual ideas and appreciations to weaken the hold of his affections upon his own country and people. His patriotism has always controlled his reason and prevented him from making any violent protest in the name of Reason against the thoughts, beliefs, traditions and institutions of his race.

Patriotism is really of two kinds, abstract and concrete. The social and religious reformer loves his country and his people as ardently and devotedly as any other person; but his patriotism is of the abstract kind. He loves only the good, the beautiful and the true, in his own country. He has no toleration for the bad, the ugly and the false. He is more or less of an iconoclast. He is cast in the mould of the prophet—rigid, uncompromising, faithful to whatever is true and good, relentless in his war against whatever, in his eyes, is false and evil.

His country is to him more of an ideality than a reality. Krishna Kumar's patriotism is essentially of this type, among us. But there is another class of patriotism also. It may be best characterised as concrete. It is not the love of an abstraction called country or nation. It loves its people in the concrete, just as they are, a mixture of both reason and unreason, of both good and bad. It loves its nation with a pure love, which sees the whole, seizes the totality, and in that totality finds an explanation for both its reason and unreason, its good and evil, and seeing both the light and the shade together, it is able to realise the proper perspective of both. It is not blind to the faults and errors, the evils and weaknesses of its own nation, but only sees their natural explanations which others fail to see, and thus recognising the spirit of truth and goodness and the source of strength that lie hidden underneath them he seeks to remove and remedy them from within, by working up the latent goodness and strength; and is in the meantime lovingly tolerant of them. This is the character of what may be called concrete patriotism. Syam Sundar's patriotism is of this kind, and consequently, it is characterised by an intense conservatism, which is the soul of natural, as distinguished from philosophic, nationalism everywhere.

But Syam Sundar is by no means a .igid and hide-bound conservative. He is always prepared to move with the times, and, in practical life, he has, like almost every Nationalist, given up many of the obsolete institutions and usages of his country and his caste. Born of very high-class Brahmin parents—his father was a well-known *Adhyapaka* or professor of Brahminical lore—he observes all the formalism of Brahminical life, to the extent that these are demanded by the public opinion of his caste. But as far as that public opinion commended to become tolerant of heterodox habits and thoughts, Syam Sundar does not refuse to follow them. In fact, he does not even shrink from initiating these reforms, provided they do not create any vital disruption in social life. He is therefore as much at home with the orthodox Brahmin-Pandit as with the heterodox England-returned civilian or Barrister.

It is neither in eating nor drinking (though he is a teetotaller) that his Brahminism ever seeks to assert itself. Neither is it in his pride of birth that it comes out. He mixes freely with all castes, and in private life treats the Pariah with almost the same respect as he would render to a Brahmin, provided, of course, the former occupies in education and character the same position as the latter. But all the inherent pride of race in the man comes out the moment when mere wealth seeks to assert itself over culture or character. In one sense, therefore Syam Sundar's spirit is perhaps the most democratic among the leading Nationalist workers in Bengal. But it is the democracy of the Brahmin, the claims of the intellect and the real man to equality, despite all differences in worldly position due to wealth or rank. It is the proud protest of the old spirit of intellectual and spiritual aristocracy of Hinduism against the British-created aristocracy of land and lucre. Along with this pride of intellect and culture, Syam Sundar has also inherited from his Brahmin ancestors a tender humanity, which is almost feminine in its care for the weak and the bereaved. Extremely sensitive to the least suspicion of slight or neglect, Syam Sundar is also among the most selfless of our public men. Very poor himself, he has never refused to part with his last penny, to any one, friend or acquaintance, who stood in greater or even equal need of it. Poverty makes misanthropes in Europe, his own poverty has made something of a philanthropist of this chip of an old and aristocratic Brahmin block. How much of it is due to his inheritance in the supremely spiritual civilisation of his nation, and how much to his own personal temperament, it is difficult to say. But whatever may be their origin and their cause, all who have come into intimate contact with Syam Sundar, have found his impulses to be almost uniformly noble, and his ideas lofty.

SRIJUT MANORANJAN GUHA-THAKURTA

Few people outside Bengal had heard of Srijut Manoranjan Guha-Thakurta, until his arrest and deportation last December, without any public indictment or trial, made his name a household word all over India. And the reason of it is that Manoranjan had never been a prominent figure in Indian politics all his life. Of about the same age as Aswini Kumar Datta, Manoranjan has been a preacher of religion. Unlike the other leaders of the Nationalists in Bengal, Manoranjan had never been to any English school. But endowed with large intellectual powers, his native talents made up very largely for his want of regular school or collegiate education. Descended from the stock of Maharaja Pratabaditya, whose glorious but tragic career represented in Bengal at the time of Akbar the same movement in Hindu nation-building in Mahomedan India, which Sivaji represented with greater success, and on a much larger and imperial scale in Maharashtra, Manoranjan belongs to one of the highest castes of Bengalee Hindus, and can claim social-precedence of every non-Brahmin British manufactured, Raja or Maharaja in the Province. Like Asvini Kumar Manoranjan also belongs to Barisal, and like him, he too came in early youth under the influence of the Brahmo Samaj, and was for some years a missionary and minister of that church. Possessing quite exceptional gifts of oratory, and fairly well-versed in the traditions and legendary lore of his people, Manoranjan was the most successful preacher of the new social and religious ideals to the masses of Bengal that the Brahmo Samaj ever had. There is a very strong community of Nama-Sudras in Barisal and the neighbouring districts of Kulna and Faridpur. Orthodox Hinduism has relegated them to an inferior social position, but they represent at the same time the finest class of peasantry in Bengal. Owing to the larger security against repeated enhancement of rents afforded by the Permanent Settlement in Bengal, these Nama-Sudras are perhaps the most prosperous of

Indian agriculturists. In some cases they even own the lands they cultivate. British policy and administration have given them a status which they never had as a caste either under the ancient Hindu or the later Mahomedan regime. All these have combined to quicken a spirit of freedom in them which constantly chafes under the social inferiority imposed by the orthodox Hindu social economy. This offers an excellent opportunity to the Christian missionaries, which they have been not slow to utilise, and increasing numbers of this caste in Barisal and the neighbouring districts were being converted to Christianity. As a missionary of the Brahmo Samaj, Manoranjan worked among these people with marked success for some time, and appreciably checked the progress of the foreign missionary propaganda among them. His social rank and position, which he had openly abjured for conscience sake, his strong common sense, his intimate knowledge of the life and thoughts of the common people, added to his natural gifts of oratory, made him very popular among people who had not received an English education and who had no familiarity with foreign ways of thought and modes of expression.

But the Brahmo Samaj could not keep him long. Like Asvini Kumar, Monaranjan also came under the influcnce of Pundit Bijoy Krishna Goswami, and gradually drifted away from the movement of the Brahmo Samaj. If the Brahmo Samaj had visibly checked the progress of Christianity among English educated Indians, the Bhakti Movement of Pundit Bijoy Krishna Goswami appreciably checked the progress of the Brahmo-Samaj among a large section of English-educated Bengalees. Pundit Bijoy Krishna was himself for the greater part of his life a missionary of the Brahmo Samaj. Descended from Advaitacharya, the contemporary and co-adjutor of Sree Chaitanya, his family had been the spiritual teachers of the Vaishnavas of Bengal for nearly four hundred years. Both by heredity and training, Pundit Bijoy Krishna had always the spirit of Vaishnavic piety in him, and if he imbibed in his early youth his rationalistic ideas from Keshub Chunder Sen, in his turn he contributed more than any one else a deeper and fervent spirituality in the movement headed by the great reformer. The Brahmo Samaj received this emotional note almost entirely from Pundit Bijoy Krishna. It was, however, unable to appreciate and accommodate the later development of this great saint and sage who had to resign his connection with this body towards the end of his life. He soon became the centre of a new movement which not only drew earnest souls within its fold from every part of Bengal, but received recognition from every class and sect of holy men all over India. At the great gathering of Hindu saints and sanyasis at Allahabad in 1896 Pundit Bijoy Krishna was received as their equal by all the men of India assembled there. Manoranjan was present at Allahabad with his master, and it was his contact and conversation with the holy men of his country, added to the inspiration of his Guru, which re-created his faith in the culture and high destiny of his race.

Pundit Bijoy Krishna's creed and philosophy were absolutely free from the reactionary spirit which characterised the general Hindu Revival of the closing years of the last century in India. These had declared open war against the liberal religious movement in the country. They sought to revive the mediæval faiths and ideas and perpetuate the current social institutions of the land. Theirs was, thus, in some sense a work of resistance, so far as modern thoughts and ideals are concerned. Pundit Bijoy Krishna's movement was, however, fundamentally different from the revivals, inasmuch as he did not deny the validity of the work of the Brahmo Samaj, with which he had himself been so prominently connected at one time, but simply pointed to a further development from which that body seemed to shrink. The Brahmo Samaj was the product of the dual influence, one being the influence of modern European illumination, which was essentially rationalistic and deistic, and the other was the influence of the ancient theosophy of the Upanishads. Theologically, its prevailing emphasis was more on what is called the Abstract Universal than on what is indicated as the Concrete Universal. The traditional Brahma-Jnan or Hindu Gnosticism more decidedly lent towards the abstract and the transcendental than towards the concrete and the eminental. It did not deny the eminental aspect of the Absolute, but relegated it to a lower place, to the realm of nescience or Avidya or Maya. All conceptions of relations implying duality warred against the monistic theory ot philosophic Hinduism, and had, therefore, to be got rid of for the apprehension of the highest reality and truth. The ultimate Reality is pure being ; it is different from all that we know and different from all that we do not know. It is not an object of our senses, neither it is an object of our mind or thought, for all thought is through the relations of subject and object, and where all relations are cancelled there all thoughts also must cease. But thought and being had been identified by some philosophers. It is, however, found at the final analysis to be only an expression of being and not the being itself. Hindu gnosticism claims experience of a state of consciousness where all thoughts cease but consciousness still remains. To ordinary man and woman thought and consciousness are one and the loss of thought means to them the loss of consciousness. They regard it as a state of unconsciousness. But to the Hindu gnostics, this loss of the sense of duality and relations means not an unconscious, but a superconscious state, not the loss, but the highest perfection of being. In this state the knower exists in his own self. He then realises the Absolute as the Absolute in his own self as his own self. But even this language is only metaphorical ; in the highest cognition of the Self there is neither in nor as. It is not knowledge, but direct realisation. It is Aparokshanubhuti, as we have it in Sanskrit—immediate cognition. It is indescribable, they say, it is unthinkable : it is known by those only who attained it. This is the last word of the Vedanta. This is the ultimate teaching of the Upanishads. This is the truth of the highest Yoga or union of the soul and the Over-Soul. So far as the Brahmo Samaj is affiliated with the ancient gnosticism of India, this is the highest theological ideal. So far as it is affiliated to modern European thought and theology, the

Brahmo Samaj is partly deistic and partly theistic in the Christian sense of the term. Like Christian Unitarianism, the logic of popular Brahmoism is essentially deistic; though like the Unitarians, in their practical devotions and piety the Brahmos also are essentially theistic. Towards the close of his life, Pundit Bijoy Krishna went beyond the theosophy of the Upanishads and the Vedanta. He did not deny the truth of the Brahmo ideal of the Brahma-jnan, or the direct and immediate divine cognition. He even accepted the negations of the Brahmo creed as a necessary stage in the progress of the soul towards true divine knowledge. But in his later life he proclaimed a higher stage, higher than the rationalism of the Brahmo Samaj and gnosticism of the Upanishads. After the Upanishads came the Puranas, after the gnosticism of the Vedanta came the gospel of love and faith of the Vaishnavas. As the theosophy of the Upanishads was an advance upon the naturalism of the Vedas, so the Concrete Universalism of the Vaishnavas came as an advance upon the abstract-Universalism of the Vedantas. Each preceding stage was a necessary moment in the evolution of each succeeding stage. Pundit Bijoy Krishna's creed and philosophy, thus summed up the highest thought and philosophy of the Hindus. It was to some extent a new synthesis of the Hindu thought of our age.

Hinduism when properly understood, represents a particular type of piety and spiritual ideal. The social economy is based upon distinctions of caste—literally colours—and orders. It is summed up by the Sanskrit expression, Varnasrama-Dharma, the law of varna and the law of asrama. The varnas are the castes, the asramas are the four social orders, the student, the householder, the retired and the mendicant ; and the aim and object of all these is to cure the individual of his conceit of individuality, to train him in the truth that his highest life is not in opposition to, but in a thorough and conscious identification with the Universal. To recognise the One in the many and to realise his own unity with the One: this is the end and aim of man's life in Hinduism in both its speculative as well as in its practical side. Strange as it may sound to the ignorant and unimaginative foreigner, the essential divinity of man is the central conception of Hinduism. And, therefore, the moment a person realises his essential divinity, his one-ness with God, he is released from all restrictions, and becomes a law unto himself. To such a man there is neither Brahmin nor Sudra. Every man and woman is a revelation of the Supreme. Should a Pariah attain this state he receives the honour to which few Brahmins are permitted to aspire.

But though this is the general characteristic of Hinduism, it is brought out more prominently in Vaishanvism than perhaps in any other sect or school. The intense humanitarianism of Pundit Bijoy Krishna, which in his younger days found expression in and through the religious revolt of the Brahmo Samaj, found, if anything, even a deeper and fuller expression in and through his later and Vaishnavic developments. As a Brahmo he had looked upon man as an equal and a brother; as a Vaishnava he now realised in every man and woman the presence and personation of his God. The message of his old Brahmoism was the brotherhood of man, which formulated itself in a propaganda of social amelioration. The message of his later Vaishnavism was the divinity of man, which transformed the service of man into a living service of God, and worked out a noble transfiguration in all human relations and social activities. Profound as was this piety, even as a member and minister of the Brahmo Samaj, it deepened with his age, until he stood before the Hindus of Bengal as an object lesson of the highest and most passionate love of God described in their scriptures and exemplified in the lives of their saints and avatars.

This saintly person, Manoranjan accepted as his Guru. To him he consecrated his life. From him he drew all the deepest inspirations of his character. Having retired from the missionary work of the Brahmo Samaj, Manoranjan continued to preach the gospel of that ardent and passionate love of God and consecrated service of man, which he saw exemplified in the character and conversation of his master.

Family bereavements added to the ascension of his Guru, compelled Manoranjan to retire from public life for a time; but the new nationalist upheaval in Bengal, following upon the ill-advised partition of that Province by Lord Curzon, brought him out of his temporary retirement and placed him among the foremost preachers of the new gospel of a free and self-regulated national life as an essential pre-condition for the realisation of the life in God of every individual member of the nation. The cry of Bande Mataram or Hail Motherland, with which this new movement started, is not a mere political formula to him. Mere politics appealed very little to this gifted Bengalee poet and preacher. Whatever politics he professes is a part of his religious ideal. And the cry of Bande Mataram was to him an inspired Mantra. His nation is to him an ordering of his God, ordained to reveal to him the love and life of his Maker. The Mother in Bande Mataram is to him not a mere poetical impersonation, but a concrete revelation of his God. Under the inspiration of the spirit of his Guru, Manoranjan now consecrated himself and all he could call his own to the service of this deity, the Mother or the Motherland.

Without, perhaps, a very clear and strong grasp of that organic conception of the social unit that has commenced to almost revolutionise ideas of our time regarding the relation between the individual and the social whole to which he belongs, which forms the fundamental basis of what we have characterised in these columns as philosophic nationalism, Manoranjan has drawn from his studies of the religious scriptures and social institutes and ideals of his nation, as strong an inspiration of the new nationalist ideals and thoughts as has been drawn by others from modern thought and culture. Accepting the teachings of his Guru, he believes that God is one, and Humanity is also one. But, at the same time, as the Divine Unity is not an undifferentiated but only a self-differentiated Unity, even so the unity of the human race is also a unity which exists in and realises itself through endless varieties, some personal and individualistic, and some racial or national and collectivistic. This conception of the fundamental difference existing as a Divine ordering among different tribes and communities of men, is a fundamental implication of all ethnic creeds and force. It is a fundamental implication of the social creed and codes of the Hindus also. Consequently, the gospel of nationalism is not an unfamiliar thing to the thoughtful Hindu acquainted with the literaturo and traditions of his people. In fact, in some sense the nationalism of the Hindu, trained and educated in Hindu ways alone, is much stronger and of greater intrinsic worth than the selfish and self-seeking, the imitative and unspiritual political antipathy which so often masquerades as fervent nationalism among us. In the case of Manoranjan, however, the spirit of nationalism, while it had its roots in the teachings and traditions of his own people, received a broader and universal outlook partly through his close and long associations with the best class of his English-educated countrymen and partly, or more correctly speaking, through the universalistic teachings of his Guru.

It is sometimes ignorantly believed that the conception of humanity is a new conception in India. And in support of this error it is pointed that neither Sanskrit nor any of the English vernaculars derived from Sanskrit has any term to express the concept humanity. Even some of our own people have lent their support to this falsehood by coining new words to express this concept. But a careful study of Vaishnavic scriptures reveals the fact that the Hindus have a much deeper conception of Humanity than what has yet been developed among the people of Europe or America. Practically, Europe recognises only one kind of humanity, which is not humanity but white-manity. Non-white races do not count as essential factors of humanity. Their amelioration may be undertaken as an act of pity, their preservation may be desirable to help the growth of the white races, but they are not an organic part and element of that humanity which the white races represent. This is the practical idea concerning Humanity among the enlightened and dominant white peoples of the modern world. The truly Christian conception of Humanity is, we know, very different from this. That conception has grown around the doctrine of Christ, as propounded in the Fourth Gospel. In a right interpretation of that doctrine, Christ and Humanity are really one. He is the Light of the world. He is the light which lighteth every man coming to the world. And as in higher Christian thought and philosophy the ideal of Humanity has grown around the conception of Logos, even so in higher Hinduism the ideal of humanity has grown around the conception of Narayana. Narayana is the In-dweller, severally in n-dividual souls, and collectively, he is also the soul, so to say, of the whole of the human race. And this dual conception of Narayana as manifested in human units and constituting the basal unity and continuity of individual life and consciousness, and as eternally revealing and realising itself—to use a Hegelian terminology—in and through the progressive evolution of the collective life and consciousness of the human race, lends a much deeper meaning and significance to the Hindu's conception of Humanity than is found anywhere outside the very highest level of Christian idealism. But the underlying monistic or pantheistic ideas of Hinduism have lent strength to the Hindu ideal of humanity both in its individual and collective aspects, which, owing to its essential dualistic emphasis Christianity has not been able to impart to it in either of these aspects.

Narayana is not a mere philosophical generalisation or a metaphysical abstraction. He is a concrete person like the Logos of orthodox Christian theology, but a person who is eternally revealing himself through innumerable human personalities, as well as who stands as the soul and spirit of the collective life of humanity. To the devout vaishnava, every man is a manifestation of Narayana. And Narayana being endowed with a divine sensorium participates, in some sense, in the enjoyment and sufferings of each individual human being. This suffering is not original but vicarious; but none the less it is a part of divine experience. Collectively, also, the privations and sufferings of the race are equally part of divine experience. In this deeper sense, the services of man—every attempt to remove his ignorance, to relieve his sufferings, and set him upon the truest and highest basis of his life—all these elements are in the worship of God. Whatever contributes to human misery, whatever retards the developments of humanity, whatever obstructs the advance of man into his proper and conscious life in God, is therefore an outrage against God Himself. Narayana is perpetually seeking to reveal and realise Himself in and through the life of each individual man and woman, and through the life of humanity. The bondage of man is in one sense the bondage of Narayana Himself. Poverty, ignorance, social repression, political servitude, are therefore as much a violation of the Dharma or the Divine Law as anger and lust and other mortal sins.

This is the general philosophy of life and duty which Manoranjan had imbibed from the teachings and character of his saintly master, and it lies at the back of all his public activities, whether as a preacher of religion or an advocate of the political and economic independence of his people. Like Asvini Kumar's and Krishna

Kumar's his politics also are a part of his religion. Like Asvini Kumar's and Krishna Kumar's his patriotism is also an expression of his general ideal of universal humanity. To him humanity is a genus; the different races and nations of the world with their special temperaments and civilisations, are different species of this genus homo. The progress and development of humanity is dependent upon the progress and development of every branch of mankind. Love of his own country means, therefore, to Manoranjan no necessary hatred of other lands and other peoples.

By nature and training, Manoranjan is incapable of wantonly causing hurt to either man or beast. The one lesson that has been almost incessantly impressed by his Guru, is that whoever wants to attain Bhakti or real love of God must cultivate kindness and pity towards all sentient creatures, and attachment to the name of the Lord. The motto of the discipline he has placed himself is :—

"With a humility that is humbler than the lowly grass which suffers to be trodden by man and beast without a protest, with a forbearance greater than that of the trees which do not withdraw their shade even from the man who comes to cut their branches and rob them of their wealth of flowers and fruits, with a spirit which never seeking honour for itself is ever ready to give preference to others, should the name of the Lord be perpetually sung."

SISTER NIVEDITA

Sister Nivedita's—otherwise known as Miss Margaret Noble—was a most *dynamic* personality. The adjective is her own in a sense, used of course in another context. She spoke once, I remember, to a large and appreciative audience in the Calcutta Town Hall, on what she called "*Dynamic Religion.*" It was a protest against the excessively speculative and quiescent emphasis of our national life and philosophy. As a disciple of Swami Vivekananda she was not unaware of the supreme value of the speculative and quiescent life of the true man of God. But the current quietude and hair-splitting speculations of the pundits are of a different type; these are not really *satvic* (सात्विक) but *tamasic* (तामसिक); represent not the calm of the highest union with the Universal, but the inertia of the spiritually dead. This quietude was no part of Nivedita's religion. It was no part of the Religion of her Master either. Religion to her was not a passive pursuit of what merely is, but an untiring and ever-vigilant effort for the realisation of what ought to be. This perpetual striving of what ought to be, constitutes the dynamic element of every religion. And it was this what Nivedita meant when she spoke to us on *Dynamic Religion*.

Born among Christian peoples, in a Christian family, Margaret Noble gradually ceased, like so many others of her class and country, to be a Christian. And it seems to me that her revolt against present-day Christianity was very largely due to the fact that it is not, in spite of all its restless efforts to make the world better than what it is, truly and rationally dynamic. In fact the inner logic of all credible religions, that claim absolute authority for the teachings of a Master who lived many centuries or many milleniums ago, and finality for a particular scheme of religious and spiritual disciplines that suited a particular people at a particular stage of their mental and social evolution, must inevitably be more or less rigidly conservative and static, and not freely progressive and dynamic. The theology of the Christian Churches prevents the free play of the human-intellect; and its ethics, owing to its excessive legalism, tends to cripple the human personality. The Jewish Jehova was more dynamic in some aspects, than the Christian Deity. Paganism was far more dynamic, than even Judaism. But Nivedita found this dynamic element of the human religion nowhere more fully realised and represented than in the Hindu Cult of the *Kalee*.

In fact, I always felt that Nivedita was, at heart a pagan of pagans. She was, literally, a child of Nature. Her love of Nature was as passionate and personal as that of the ancient Greeks. I never found another moderner, man or woman, in India or Europe though I have heard of some Hindu devotees of this type, whose whole being, body and mind and soul, seemed to be so completely attuned to the life of the outer elements. Her whole system appeared to me to have been uniformly responsive to the moods of the nature-forces about her.

Once I was sitting with Nivedita in her house in Bosepara Lane, sipping tea out of her quaint swadeshi cups. Suddenly the sky was overcast with black scowling clouds as oftentimes happens in our early summer evenings; and there was immediately a marked change in the mood of my hostess. Her face seemed at once to reflect this awfully dynamic mood of nature. It beamed with a new light, at once awful and lovely. And she sat silent, apparently unconscious for the moment of my presence, looking intently through the window at the gathering gloom about the earth and the heavens, and listening like one in a trance, to the rising tumult of the growing storm. And just as there came in a little while the first flash of lightning followed by the crash of the first thunder, she cried out with bated breath—*Kalee*.

It was then that I understood for the first time what it really was that had drawn this essentially pagan woman, born by some mischance among Christian peoples, to our country and to our culture. Nivedita so enthusiastically accepted the cult of our Kalee because she found here the most perfect representation of what may be called the Nature-Religion. Modern scientific education as distinguished from strict scientific training, when joined to highly poetic temperaments, creates this Nature-Religion in our age. Nivedita's was a highly poetic temperament. She had received considerable scientific education. And these two combined to create her personal religion also.

Her scientific education had killed on the one hand, her faith in the Abstraction which ordinary Christianity calls its God, and had on the other strengthened her hold on the realities of the Natural Order. But, even the nature of the scientist is after all an abstraction. Science knows actually the cause and conditions of what are called natural phenomena: but neither lens nor lancet can reveal the totality of these multitudinous manifestations, which the man of science spells as Nature with a capital N. The scientists' Nature, even though it may somewhat satisfy the cravings of the intellect, can never meet the requirements of the aesthetic and emotional life. These needs can be met only by an idealisation of Nature, both in its disjunctive and its collective aspect, which must be at once poetic and spiritual. Greek naturalism very largely achieved this at one time. Pagan religion and Pagan art are both so charming because of their close and living relations with Nature, not in the abstract but in the concrete, not as a generalisation of thought but as something that could be touched and tasted, seen and loved, as a sensuous object, and which was yet not purely of the senses. Our enjoyment of form for instance is through the senses and not sensuous. So also of sound in music. And this supersensuous element on these clearly sensuous experiences and enjoyments comes from the emotions with which we must paint every sensuous object before we can draw any pleasure out of them. The charm of paganism lay thus in this subtle blending of the poetical and the spiritual with the sensuous and the materialistic, in its religious and art life. Thus even the supernatural in paganism was intensely natural. And Nivedita before she came in contact with Vivekananda, must have, I think, built her inner soul-life upon these ancient inheritances of the modern Christian civilisation.

But Paganism is dead, stone dead without any hope or possibility of a resurrection. There is no life in the ancient ruins and relics of Greece and Rome. They are no longer sources of inspiration to living men. In our study and appreciation of these we have to fall back, perforce, upon our own historic or poetic imagination, and thus possibly shut ourselves more or less from the stern actualities of our present life and environments, and transfer ourselves, as in a pleasant dream, to the long-buried past. To study and understand these we must largely depend upon our own subjectivity for they do not exist objectively for us. Apollo or Aphrodite, Jupiter and Juno, are all dead—they and all their devoted worshippers, who in their own life and conversation brought them out in concrete shapes before their contemporaries. We do not see before our eyes what these great gods and goddesses could actually have been to those who looked upon them not as interesting archaelogical relics or invaluable art treasures, but actual beings, all-knowing and omnipotent, who punished their foes and rewarded their friends, and could receive and indeed, though apparently without life or sentiency, who did even reciprocate, the love and devotion of their worshippers. We always and everywhere see and know and understand and appreciate and realise the life and the love of God in and through the life and love of his devotees. This is the true meaning of the text: "He who has seen the son has seen the father." We thus know Christ not by or in the Gospels, but in and through his revelation in the life and conversation of the true Christian. The Christian who does not make his Christ manifest in his own thought and life has no title to the name. We know our own Krishna, not from the Mahabharata or the Sreemad Bhagabat, neither from the Geeta nor from the Harivamsa, or any other Vaishnava Puranas but from the living Vaishnava, who in his life and activities reproduces, as upon the face of a mirror, the life and love of his Master, or Friend or Lover. It is the same everywhere. The devotees of every cult are the only true, living, soulful and the intelligible interpretation of that cult. A religion that exists only in papyrus or inscriptions, in stone and clay or bronze, in archaelogical ruins or time-worn relics, is not a living but a dead religion. We can only seek to understand it by putting our own meanings upon its dogmas and rituals, and even to study it scientifically in the light of psychological generalisations of universal human experience in regard to matters pertaining to human religion, but can never see face to face what it must have meant or stood for, to those that personally practised that extinct religion at one time. The ancient Nature-Religion of Greece and Rome is extinct, absolutely killed by Christianity, and even the enaissance has not been able to resurrect it. The modern pagan, consequently, can find absolutely no help from the literature or art of the ancient Pagan world, to reconstruct his own personal religion. Neither Nivedita nor any one else who in our age may have imbibed partly through their scientific and partly through their artistic education the old spirit of the Pagan Religions, could possibly find any help from the records or relics of Paganism to fully and rationally interpret this spirit to their own reason and experience. Nivedita, in any case, found the thing that she had evidently been longing for, in the religion of the Hindus as it is being pursued and lived by countless numbers in India, and as it was first interpreted to her by Swami Vivekananda. And here she found indeed a good deal more than what could be found—I do not say in the Philosophy of Greece—but decidedly in either the Greek or the Roman religion. But of this I cannot speak in this short notice of this small book.

For the present I would only say that in a small but intensely interesting volume we get a glimpse of the inner character of Nivedita's soul, more perhaps than in any other of her books. Her object in these pages was not really to portray herself, but rather to study and understand her Master. It is Vivekananda here and Vivekanada there, and Vivekananda all over. These pages were not written originally, I think, for the public eye. These are jottings of Nivedita's thoughts and impressions of what were clearly the most momentous days of her life. It was, I think, during her first visit to India, that she went about the Himalayas, at Nainital and Almora, and Cashmere with Vivekananda and his party; and these pages are her private record of that pilgrimage. And they show how gradually the spirit of her Master possessed her, and through his life and love she was able to see India and her peoples, her thoughts and institutions, her religion and her rituals, in a light such as had never been vouchsafed before to any foreigner. Here the devoted disciple, lost in the Love of the Master, in trying to preserve the sacred recollections of his words, incidentally paints also her own innermost soul, a painting which is the more faithful and fascinating because it is absolutely unconscious. It is a beautiful picture of Vivekananda in Nivedita, and Nivedita in Vivekananda; the Master in the Disciple and the Disciple in the Master;—the Two thus made One.

P. R. RAMA IYAR AND CO., PRINTERS, MADRAS